BUILDING STRATEGIC ORGANIZATIONS
The First Five Tools of Strategy and Strategic Planning

BUILDING STRATEGIC ORGANIZATIONS

The First Five Tools

of Strategy and Strategic Planning

Rick Mann, PhD

Building Strategic Organizations:
The First Five Tools of Strategy and Strategic Planning
By Rick Mann, PhD

Published by: ClarionStrategy LLC, Nashville, TN
www.ClarionStrategy.com

DEDICATION

To an ever-growing number of
strategic leaders around the world

TABLE OF CONTENTS

ClarionToolBox Series

Strategic Leaders Are Made, Not Born: The First Five Tools for Escaping the Tactical Tsunami

Building Strategic Organizations: The First Five Tools of Strategy and Strategic Planning

Enterprise Leaders: The First Five FIELD Tools (coming 2020)

Strategic Finance for Strategic Leaders: The First Five Tools (coming 2021)

ACKNOWLEDGMENTS

I'd like to begin by thanking all of the strategic organizations that I have had the privilege of working with over the years.

I also want to thank the Trevecca Nazarene University leaders who have encouraged me to research, write, consult and coach throughout my faculty tenure. These include the Dean of the Skinner School of Business and Technology, Jim Hiatt; the University Provost, Tom Middendorf; and the University President, Dan Boone.

Also, many thanks to my editor, Kara de Carvalho, and my graphic designer, Lieve Maas of Bright Light Graphics, who have been invaluable in the development of this book.

Lastly, I want to thank my wife, Cheri, who has supported my work in so many ways.

PREFACE

People everywhere want to build strategic organizations that will make the world a better place. Welcome to the journey of building strategic organizations. You may be a veteran of this process, or you may be early in your career and wondering how all this works. Either way, I suggest that you read my book, *Strategic Leaders Are Made, Not Born: The First Five Tools for Escaping the Tactical Tsunami.* These five tools provide a foundation for the five tools presented in this book. Even if you are an experienced builder of strategic organizations, you might find these two volumes helpful for developing the strategic capacity of your entire workforce. We want to change the world, and strategic organizations are one of the ways to do that. In order for that to happen, we need more people who can think, lead, and consult effectively to that end.

We know that most people work and lead at the tactical level. We also know that when organizations function primarily at the tactical level, they fail to reach their full potential.

Leaders of strategic organizations have greater clarity on where they are going, their most important priorities, and how they are doing.

Leaders of strategic organizations have greater clarity on where they are going, their most important priorities, and how they are doing.

Strategic organizations do not arise by chance. The process requires clarity and commitment, along with sound strategy and execution. This book can help you and your team maximize the value you create for your important stakeholders.

Over the years, I have worked through these processes with dozens of organizations. This book is an attempt to put together the thinking of world-class strategic thought leaders, along with some practical principles that will hopefully help you to help others.

BUILDING STRATEGIC PERSONAL AND PROFESSIONAL LIVES

Most people have goals that go beyond building strategic organizations. They have hopes for their lives, their families, and for their professional work. The good news is that everything we talk about here can be applied personally, professionally, and organizationally. I call this the "PPO approach." I use the PPO approach in all of my books and graduate courses because my goal is for you to apply every tool that you learn at the following levels:

- Personal
- Professional
- Organizational

Clay Christensen, a professor at Harvard Business School and the acclaimed author of the *Innovator's Dilemma* (1997), details the PPO approach in his book, *How Will You Measure Your Life?* (2012). I have my MBA students read his 6-page *Harvard Business Review* article (2010) by the same title, while my DBA students read the full book.

My hope for you is that you can win at life *and* win at work. The result can be a flourishing personal and family life as well as a thriving organization.

Recently, I was very encouraged on this front. I had just spent several hours with 25 leaders from around the world going over the content of *Strategic Leaders Are Made, Not Born*. These leaders were the VPs and the most important directors of a global organization. At the end of our time together, the group's leader asked each person to share something that they felt was most meaningful. About five of the leaders shared how they planned to use the tools from the book with their adult children. I couldn't have been happier. While I want their organization to be successful, I am more concerned that they win at home and in life by using the PPO approach.

FOR-PROFITS AND NONPROFITS ARE MORE SIMILAR THAN DIFFERENT

When I was president of Crown College in Minnesota, a multi-million-dollar nonprofit, and was considering getting my MBA, I thought that for-profits and nonprofits were quite different. The further along the journey I go, the more similarities I see between the two. The desire to create value for its stakeholders lies at the heart of every company and organization.

Similarly, both need money to operate. For-profits get money from investors and customers. Nonprofits also get money from investors (usually called donors) and often, but not always, from customers. For example, Fortune 500 companies have investors (stockholders) and customers (think of Target and Delta). Nonprofits have investors (think of large donors like Bill Gates and small donors like you and me) as well as customers (such as college students and hospital patients). Lastly, some nonprofits only have donors because their end-users are not paying customers.

The desire to create value for its stakeholders lies at the heart of every company and organization.

In summary, I have found that for-profits are looking for a cause to support (like nonprofits), while nonprofits are looking for more effective and efficient processes (like for-profits).

The principles outlined in this book can be applied to all kinds of teams, organizations, and companies, regardless of whether they are for-profits or nonprofits.

INTRODUCTION

You can be that person. You can be the consultant who helps others build a strategic organization. Sure, you may not currently have a consultant's title, office, income, or even experience. Nonetheless, organizations around the world need both internal and external as well as formal and informal consultants and leaders who can help them get better at what they do. In many cases, they also want to grow larger than they are so that they can extend their impact to the world around them.

While you may never serve as a stand-alone consultant, you can still help your team, organization, and others get better at what they do, whether you are a senior leader, mid-level staff, or even a board member. What does it take for you to lead and serve in this way? Let's look at some different levels of engagement.

Beginners: If you are just starting, learn the foundational concepts, ask questions, and listen well. In a year or two, you can make considerable progress in developing your consulting voice.

Intermediates: If you are an experienced team leader, take the tools you have and add to them. Build your team's strategic capacity by practicing these key tools. Also, if you have not already done so, begin to look for places where you can help other teams, departments, and organizations with their strategy work.

Advanced: If you have an established track record of consulting with others, continue to hone your craft. Think through your portfolio of duties and consider ways you could expand your strategy practice inside and outside your organization.

Grad Students: Maybe you are reading this as a grad student and are not sure where to go with it all. In these 100 or so pages, we can get you up and creating value for others. It doesn't matter whether you are shy or outgoing—you can get started and keep moving. Who knows where you might end up?

Building a strategic organization takes time, focus, teamwork, and intentionality. We will look at what it means to build a strategic organization from the top-down as well as from the bottom-up.

Building a strategic organization takes time, focus, teamwork, and intentionality.

You have probably known the satisfaction of building something. It could be a model airplane with your kids, a new house, or a transformational organization. I have had the joy of partnering with leaders, programs, and organizations that go on to bring significant transformations to the lives of people around the world.

Let's work together to build something great as we explore some important tools for building strategic programs and organizations. With these tools, you and others can accelerate the development of strategic organizations.

Over the decades, I have built a number of organizations and programs, ranging from start-ups to significant expansions. These have included:

- A college
- An MBA program
- A DBA program (start-up)
- A global coaching network (start-up)
- A domestic executive coaching program (start-up)
- A congregation
- A church plant (start-up)

- A consulting firm (start-up)
- A Chinese language program (start-up)
- An organization's publishing division (start-up)
- A nursing program (start-up)

This book highlights principles from building these programs and organizations as a way to walk you through the five tools of building strategic organizations. I introduce additional material from other programs and organizations I have helped to build over the past 20-plus years. Lastly, I include the insights that have come from helping dozens of organizations with this process.

CREATING VALUE: THE HEART OF STRATEGY

There is a reason why creating value shows up first in these books and frameworks:

- *Strategic Leaders Are Made, Not Born* (Rick Mann)
- *The Personal MBA* (Josh Kaufman)
- *What Management Is* (Joan Magretta)
- Porter's Five Tests of Good Strategy (Michael Porter)

Value creation is the heart, soul, and engine of good strategy work. The goal of every organization is to create value for its stakeholders. Value refers to the benefits that a person or an organization provides to others. Let's make sure that throughout this book and in our lives, we keep creating value central.

The goal of every organization is to create value for its stakeholders.

A simple example would be a good friend who creates value for you by listening well and being supportive and encouraging. In the business world, value creation can be quantified. When Amazon's CEO, Jeff Bezos, helped grow the company's market cap from $186B in 2014 to $400B in 2017, you could say that he created over $200B of additional financial value for Amazon stockholders in three years. When I came to Trevecca in 2013, there were just two MBA starts per year. By 2018, through the effective partnership of academics, advising, and enrollment, we had expanded to about a dozen starts per year to create greater value for the university, its students, and the community.

Once again, as you work through the material in this book, never forget that creating value for stakeholders is always at the heart of good strategy work.

FIVE STRATEGIC FOUNDATIONS

Before we launch into the five tools for strategy work, let's look at the five foundational aspects of strategy that will help support these tools including:

- Strategic Altitude
- Strategic Thinking
- Strategic Clarity
- Strategic Capacity
- Strategic Narrative

Please note that none of these five foundations mention strategic planning. In recent decades, we have moved away from strategic planning as the starting point. Instead, we begin by building strategic thinking, clarity, and capacity and then moving to strategic planning. Later in this introduction, I offer a brief history of strategic planning that outlines the process of moving from strategic planning as a process to strategic thinking.

STRATEGIC ALTITUDE

If you have read my book, *Strategic Leaders Are Made, Not Born,* you worked through the chapter on Strategic Altitude, which includes these three levels:

- Visionary Level (The **Why**)
- Strategic Level (The **How**)
- Tactical Level (The **What**)

In *Strategic Leaders Are Made,* these three levels were primarily applied at the personal and professional levels. In this book, we will see how all three of these levels come into play for organizations.

Here is a simple illustration to get you started in understanding strategic altitude. "Strategic" is shaded because it is often the most under-developed. I refer to this as the "strategy gap."

Visionary Level

The visionary level is the highest level of an organization and includes "**why**" you exist (mission), a picture of your preferred future (vision), your identity (values), and your value propositions. These high-level elements are critical to understanding who you are as an organization, what you care about, and where you are headed.

Strategic Level

If vision is about why you exist, the direction of your organization, and your preferred future, the strategic level is about "**how**" you are going to advance that vision. The strategic level includes themes, objectives, measures, and resources that are at the core of strategy development.

- **Strategic Themes** – The 1-4 areas you will focus on over the next 1-3 years.
- **Strategic Objectives** – The goal here is to craft 2-5 objectives or strategies that will advance each theme.
- **Strategic Measures** – These numbers provide clarity on strategic progress and answer the question, "How are we doing?"
- **Strategic Initiatives** – You want to align your resources and work with your strategy. Every initiative or project you undertake is made up of TEMP resources (Time, Energy, Money, and People).

Tactical Level

The tactical level is "**what**" you do on the ground as you align your daily work and resources with your vision and objectives.

Every organization needs strategic leaders who can help it to function strategically and effectively at all three altitudes.

In strategy work and strategic planning, all three levels are critical to maximizing your effectiveness. To that end, begin at the highest, visionary level. You will then move down through strategic elements, including themes, objectives, measures, and initiatives. Lastly, move from the strategic level to the tactical level as you look at the use of resources and the development of the initiatives and projects that are an essential part of your on-the-ground work.

STRATEGIC THINKING

Strategic thinking supports good strategy work and contemporary strategic planning. Strategic thinking does not begin with problem solving or strategic planning. Instead, strategic thinking takes a step back. On this, Julia Sloan, author of *Learning to Think Strategically* (2014), writes:

> The purpose of strategic thinking is to **suspend** problem-solving and **engage** in a rigorous process of examination, exploration, and **challenge** of the underlying premise of the strategy; and to **generate** new options as a means to creating a winning, innovative, and sustainable **strategy**. (Chapter 4, para. 2)

Asking the right questions and being a good listener are central to strategic thinking. What are the critical questions facing your organization? What do you hear people saying? These core skills will develop your strategic thinking. Strategic thinking is essential for all strategic leaders because it helps them see the bigger picture and ask the larger, more important questions.

Asking the right questions and being a good listener are central to strategic thinking.

STRATEGIC CLARITY

Strategic clarity is when people across the organization have good-to-great clarity on:

- **Why** do we come to work? (mission, vision, and values)
- **How** are we going to advance our organization's vision by choosing specific priorities? (strategic themes)
- **How** are we doing? (measures)
- **What** initiatives are we going to invest in that will move us forward? (resources)

Years ago, I did sabbatical research on this topic and found that senior teams often lack great clarity. Clarity continues to decrease as one moves down through the organization. As a result, most people in most organizations have insufficient strategic clarity.

Most people in most organizations have insufficient strategic clarity.

When leaders and employees lack strategic clarity, the workforce's engagement is less than ideal. The result is under-performance and a scattered array of priorities. Working through this book can help bring greater clarity to all involved.

STRATEGIC CAPACITY

Strategic capacity relates to how many employees can think and engage strategically in their work. Hughes et al. (2014) write:

Increasingly, organizations are calling on people at <u>all levels</u> to be strategic. Even if you have not heard that you need to be more strategic, we bet you can think of others with whom you work who need to develop their strategic capabilities. (p. 9)

In a related vein, Beatty (2010) asserts that:

Statistics show that fewer than 10% of leaders exhibit strategic skills, a woefully inadequate number considering the demands on organizations today....The job of strategy is not limited to a few top executives. **Strategic leaders are needed throughout our organizations** if they are to adapt, innovate and succeed well into the future. (para. 1)

The purpose of this book is to help build strategic **thinking**, strategic **clarity**, and strategic **capacity** across your organization at every level, which can in turn lead to more effective performance.

Sometimes, clients insist that they can do this on their own–and they are right. Anyone can read leading strategists like Michael Porter and John Bryson. Here are a few of their most important books:

Michael Porter
- *Competitive Advantage* (592 pages)
- *Competitive Strategy* (397 pages)
- *Understanding Michael Porter* (Joan Magretta) (256 pages)

John Bryson
- *Strategic Planning* (576 pages)
- *Creating Your Strategic Plan* Workbook (288 pages)
- *Implementing and Sustaining Your Strategic Plan* Workbook (320 pages)

These six volumes total over 2,400 pages. I suggest that you and your team begin by reading *Strategic Leaders Are Made, Not Born* and this short book and start putting them into action. As time and interest allow, you can progress to other works.

Along this journey, I will highlight some of the best strategy and strategic planning thinking and tools put forward by top strategy thinkers, including:

- Michael Porter
- John Bryson
- Clay Christensen
- John Kotter
- Richard Rumelt
- Robert Kaplan and David Norton
- Roger Martin
- Henry Mintzberg
- Jim Collins
- Thought leaders at the acclaimed Center for Creative Leadership, including Richard Hughes, Katherine Beatty, and David Dinwoodie.

STRATEGIC NARRATIVE

You can better understand strategy work if you think of it as a story. Indeed, every strategic chapter is a part of a larger story. You can begin by reflecting on where you and your team have been. Then, look at where you are. Finally, you can look ahead to where you want to go. This strategic narrative not only helps you formulate a clearer narrative of your story thus far, it can also help you and your leaders tell the story of your preferred future.

*You can better understand strategy work
if you think of it as a story.*

For example, when I arrived at Crown College to serve as Vice President of Academic Affairs in 2000, it was helpful to look back at where the College had been over the previous 80+ years. We then looked at where we were in the current marketplace. Lastly, we looked forward to where we wanted it to go in the coming years.

When I arrived at Trevecca, a Christian university in the heart of Nashville, in 2013, I listened to the business faculty talk about where they had been. Trevecca had a long history of providing access to business students who did not have the time or the money to attend neighboring Vanderbilt University full-time. However, the university did not offer its MBA program online. With a vision to providing greater access to more students, we added an online version of the MBA program. Over the next five years, we went from starting two new MBA groups each year to starting 12-15 new MBA groups each year. We needed to see Trevecca's history of providing non-traditional access to students and then continue that narrative by adding online opportunities. As of 2019, about two-thirds of Trevecca's MBA students take the program online.

These strategic narratives help us connect structured planning with the hearts and minds of our constituencies. They can also help motivate people to grow, change, and perhaps even give to an exciting future.

The strategic narrative is the **organic** and human story of the organization. Strategy and strategic planning are part of the **organized** path forward.

What Do We Do at ClarionStrategy?

When people ask us what we do at ClarionStrategy, I tell them that we are strategy coaches and consultants who invest our time:

- Building the **strategic capacity** of teams and leaders.
- Helping those leaders work through the key pieces of **strategy and strategic planning**.
- Moving them and their larger teams toward **empowerment and independence** so they can continue these processes on their own.

At ClarionStrategy, we are passionate about equipping your team to think strategically and effectively carry out the basics of good strategy and strategic planning.

STRATEGIC SPEED

Many people talk about the need for speed in today's world. We want to make sure that we do not confuse strategic speed with being tactically rushed. As I discuss in *Strategic Leaders Are Made, Not Born,* the goal is not to do more tactical work faster. The goal is to advance what you care about most. Many busy people working 12-hour days do not have strategic clarity on 1) why people should come to work, 2) their 2-3 strategic priorities, and 3) how progress is coming along.

You and your team can work through all five of these strategy levels in less than a week. In most situations where collaboration is important, you may need a few months. The goal here is not to go fast, but rather to work systematically through important strategic elements in a timely fashion.

A BRIEF HISTORY OF STRATEGY AND STRATEGIC PLANNING

Strategy work can be traced back to ancient days and to great warriors like King David in the Old Testament and Sun Tzu in China. For our purposes here, we will just focus on the decades after 1945. While strategy work emerged from the Second World War, it came into its own beginning in the 1960s.

Strategic Plan – The **Product**

In the early days, the strategic plan was the prized product of strategic planning. I have worked with many organizations that have an inch-thick plan or even a 2-inch-thick plan. Such plans take hundreds of hours to develop and can be burdensome to execute.

While those thick plans may be necessary for building airports and nuclear power plants, they are too complex and slow for most teams and organizations today. Too often, such plans spend the majority of their lives on someone's shelf.

Strategic Planning – The **Process**

Over time, people began to realize that the strategic plan should not be the focal point but rather the collaborative process that goes into making the plan. As we mentioned earlier, John Bryson (2011), a leading expert on strategic planning, writes:

> A key point to be emphasized again and again: the important activities are strategic thinking, acting, and learning, **not strategic planning per se.** Indeed, if any particular approach to strategic planning gets in the way of strategic thought, action, and learning, that planning approach should be scrapped! (p. 2)

When it comes to the process, it is invaluable to 1) identify a team of key leaders, 2) build their strategy capacity, and 3) work through the tools found in this book.

Strategic Thinking – The **People**

In today's world of rapid change, thick plans and cumbersome processes can't keep up with the pace of change and organizational needs. Now, the focus is increasingly on developing the strategic thinking of leaders at every level.

> Strategic leaders propel their organizations through successive **iterations** of a **learning** process with strategic **thinking**, strategic **acting**, and strategic **influencing** skills. These skills are needed in every element of the **learning** process, and leaders at every level in the organization can practice them. (Hughes et al., 2013, p. 4)

The purpose of this short book is to build the capacity of leaders to:

- Think strategically
- Process strategic planning collaboratively
- Document planning as needed

This lean, agile process is well within the grasp of almost every leader and team.

THE WHY, HOW, AND WHAT FRAMEWORK

As I mentioned in *Strategic Leaders Are Made, Not Born*, I draw on some of the material from the Golden Circle model popularized by Simon Sinek, the author of *Start With Why (2009)*. As of 2019, his TED talk on this subject was the 4th most-watched TED talk and counts over 40 million views. In his work, Sinek talks about three circles: **Why, How,** and **What**. He expounds on why companies do what they do. He then discusses how companies do what they do. Lastly, he talks about what companies do. I have adapted this thinking to my work here, following the same outline for each of the five tools listed in this book.

- **WHY It Matters** – First, we look at why the tool matters. This includes the importance of understanding the concepts and putting them into practice. I also explain why things go poorly when the tool is neglected.
- **HOW It Works** – Next, we unpack the main concepts that are central to the particular tool.
- **WHAT To Do Next?** – Lastly, I suggest how you can put the tool to use in your personal life, your professional life, and your organizational life (PPO).

This simple "why, how, and what" framework can help you learn and apply each tool more quickly.

WORKING MORE IS NOT THE GOAL

Nearly every organization has people who work hard. Working hard is not the goal. The goal is to increase your return on invested resources (ROI)– your limited amounts of time, energy, money, and people (TEMP)–without overworking people in the process. As a leader, your objective is not push your people to put in more hours, but rather for your organization to be more effective.

1.

CLARIFYING MISSION AND V6

"If you don't know where you are going,
any road will get you there."

—Lewis Carroll,
Alice in Wonderland

A great place for any team or organization to start is at the top. As you work through these seven elements, ask good questions and listen well. To get things headed in the right direction, begin by asking for clarification on your organization's mission and these six different Vs at the visionary level, including:

- Vision
- Values
- Value Proposition(s)
- Vector
- Voice
- Visuals

WHY IT MATTERS

Before building out its strategic level features, every organization must decide on its features at the visionary level, including mission and the first three Vs—vision, values, and value propositions. When senior leaders don't have clarity on these important visionary elements, everyone loses. The organization loses its high-level compass, while people lose the alignment that they could have had. You owe it to the people who work in your organization to gain good-to-great clarity on these important visionary-level elements. Clarity will help you and your organization perform at your best.

HOW IT WORKS

Organizational leaders can begin by working down through the essential high-level visionary elements. This is best done in collaboration with other key leaders and stakeholders.

Mission and the First 3 Vs

Most leaders are familiar with mission, vision, and values. We will start with these pieces and add the third "V," Value Propositions, resulting in the following list:

- Mission
- Vision
- Values
- Value Proposition(s)

These four elements are the main focus of the visionary level and answer the important questions of: Who are we? Where are we headed? What do we care about most? What do we provide to whom and at what cost? Any employee should be able to answer these questions with reasonable clarity.

Mission – **Why** Do You Exist? (Purpose)

Most organizations have a foundational mission statement that states the **purpose** of and the reason for their existence. Mission statements often open with phrases like, "We **exist** to…" Mission statements focus on what the organization provides:

- Our hospital exists to provide care for the under-served.
- Our company exists to provide high-quality IT services.
- Our organization exists to provide educational services for preschool children.

Ideally, mission statements provide an organization with cohesiveness and guidance. On this, Stephen Covey (1999) writes,

> An organizational mission statement—one that truly reflects the deep shared vision and values of everyone within that organization—creates a great unity and tremendous commitment. It creates in people's hearts and minds a frame of reference, a set of criteria or guidelines, by which they will govern themselves. (p. 143)

Here are some mission statements to review:

- **Teach for America**: "Growing the movement of leaders who work to ensure that kids growing up in poverty get an excellent education."
- **TED**: "Spreading Ideas"
- **Habitat for Humanity**: "Seeking to put God's love into action, Habitat for Humanity brings people together to build homes, communities, and hope."
- **March of Dimes**: "We help moms have full-term pregnancies and research the problems that threaten the health of babies."

Some organizations have either a mission statement or a vision statement, while others have both. In recent years, many organizations have moved toward a focus on vision statements, which are often shorter and more memorable. They may have a mission statement, but their vision statement lies at the forefront.

Vision – **Where** Are You Headed? (Direction)

Vision statements are usually a mix of inspirational, aspirational, and future-oriented. Your vision statement can provide direction and a picture of a preferred future. Here are some examples:

- Our vision is to see healthcare provided in the Chicagoland area.
- Our vision is a world without polio.
- Our vision is to have the highest airline market share in Thailand.

In their HBR article, "Building Your Company's Vision," Jim Collins and Jerry Porras (1996) write:

> A well-conceived vision consists of two major components: *core ideology* and *envisioned future* [...] Core ideology, the yin in our scheme, defines what we stand for and why we exist. Yin is unchanging and complements yang, the envisioned future. The envisioned future is what we aspire to become, to achieve, to create—something that will require significant change and progress to attain. (p. 3)

Some say that a vision statement describes how the world would be different if the mission were accomplished.

Here are some actual vision statements to consider:

- **Southwest Airlines:** "To become the world's most loved, most flown, and most profitable airline."

- **Teach for America:** "One day, all children in this nation will have the opportunity to attain an excellent education."
- **IKEA:** "Our vision is to create a better everyday life for many people."
- **NIKE:** "Bring inspiration and innovation to every athlete* in the world. (*If you have a body, you are an athlete)."
- **Habitat for Humanity:** "A world where everyone has a decent place to live."
- **ClarionStrategy:** "Building Strategic Leaders and Organizations."

As you look at your vision statement for review or development, here are some features to keep in mind:

- Future-focused: We imagine a day…
- Aspirational: We want to be the best at…
- Memorable: Will most of your people remember it?
- Short and concise: Less than 15 words

Vision Statements, Brand Lines/Slogans, and Tag-lines

Many organizations adopt statements that are short and memorable. A 2018 blog post on *Superbase* does an excellent job of outlining these elements:

Motel 6 Brand Line or Slogan: "Lowest price of any national chain."

Motel 6 Tagline: "We'll Leave the Light On For You"

Motel 6 Mission or Vision Statement: "To become the universally recognized leader in economy lodging. We continuously strive to reinvent the economy lodging category while remaining 100 percent committed to delivering a great experience to our guests, team members, franchisees, and partners."

Nike Brand Line or Slogan: "Authentic athletic performance"
Nike Tagline: "Just Do It"
Nike Mission or Vision Statement: "To bring inspiration and innovation to every athlete in the world."

Values – Who Are You and What Do You Care About? (Identity)

Values relate to what you care about and how you describe your identity. A person, team, organization, or company could have the following values:

- Environmental sustainability
- Empowering women
- Growing larger
- Higher profits over more substantial growth or market share

Some organizations' value statements are very long. You can have 3 to 10 or more values, but people find more than five difficult to remember. Count the number of words in your mission, vision, and value statements. Some organizations have vision and value statements that total just ten words. It is OK to have more than that, but once you get past 20 words, it will be hard to remember. For public use, consider using just a vision statement and a short set of values.

Here are some examples of value statements:

- L.L. Bean: "Sell good merchandise at a reasonable profit, treat your customers like human beings, and they will always come back for more"

- Wegmans Food Markets "Who We Are" Values
  - Caring
  - High Standards
  - Making a Difference
  - Respect
  - Empowerment

- NIKE
  - Inspiration
  - Innovation
  - Every Athlete in the World
  - Authentic
  - Connected
  - Distinctive

- ClarionStrategy
  - Developing People
  - Empowering Women and Minorities
  - Delivering Greater Value
  - Lower Costs
  - Research-Based Ideas

Value Propositions – What Do You Provide to Whom and at What Price/Cost?

While this "V" is critical to the success of any organization, it is often neglected or missing. The reason for this is simple. Many teams follow this process:

1. Mission – Why do we exist? What do we provide?
2. Vision – Where are we headed?
3. Values – What do we care about? What is our identity?
4. Let's get to work…[KC3]

Some strategy experts argue that your value proposition is the most important statement you make. Renowned strategy expert Michael Porter calls the value proposition the "first test of strategy":

> Strategy's first test, having **a distinctive value proposition**, is so intuitive that many managers think they have a strategy if they can get this far. Choosing the particular kind of value you will offer your customers is the core of competing to be unique. (Magretta, 2012, p. 95)

Value propositions answer the question: **What** do **you** provide to **others**, and at what **price/cost**?

We see four essential elements here:

- **Who** are you? Here, focus on the "you" and your self-awareness concerning your core competencies. Ask yourself: "What do we provide that others value?" A discussion of this can be found in Chapter 1 of *Strategic Leaders Are Made, Not Born.*
- Who are the **others** (stakeholders)? This question focuses on the "who"—the markets you serve. Do you sell to high-income (luxury products/services) or lower-income (value products/services) markets? For more on stakeholders, see Chapter 3 of *Strategic Leaders Are Made, Not Born.*
- **What** do you provide of value personally, professionally, or organizationally? What are the benefits of your product or services for the buyer?
- **Price/Cost**? Price is external and relates to what you charge customers in the marketplace. Cost is internal and relates to the internal expenditures needed to provide a product or service.

At times, organizations need to review and change their mission and 3 Vs. This happened during Satya Nadella's first year as CEO of Microsoft. Simone Stolzoff (2019) tells the story in his article, "How do you turn around the culture of a 130,000-person company? Ask Satya Nadella."

> At 6:02 am Pacific time, five and a half months after he took over as CEO, Nadella sent out an email with Microsoft's new raison d'être.

> Microsoft existed to "empower every person and every organization on the planet to achieve more." Though vague enough to deserve a place in the pantheon of corporate sweet nothings, the new mission offered a semantic shift that would define Microsoft for the five years that followed: It would become a people company instead of a product company. (para. 23)

Since Nadella became CEO in 2014, he has grown Microsoft's market cap by about $550B ($350B to $900B / 257%) in five years. At the end of 2018, Microsoft passed Apple to become the most valuable company in the world (by market cap).

Mission, vision, values, and value propositions are the starting place for any organization. Take time individually or organizationally to think through, talk through, and work through these elements so that you have good-to-great clarity on them. Next, work through your communication strategies, which will result in understanding and ownership of these critical elements across your entire team.

The Next 3 Vs

Mission, vision, values, and value propositions are the main elements at the visionary level. There are three other Vs that can also help give shape to any organization or company.

Vector – Where Are You Going and at What Pace?

This "V" answers the following three questions:

- Where are you? Describe your current position.
- Where are you going and what direction are you moving toward?
- At what pace or speed are you moving forward?

For example, Target could say, "We are in the US, but we would like to grow overseas at a rate of 10% per year." (On a personal note, it is interesting that when I go to Beijing, I am often in walking distance of several Walmarts. By contrast, Target has no overseas presence and shuttered its 133 Canadian stores in 2015). It is much easier to discuss a vector than it is to make it happen. Your vector needs to align with your overall vision and strategy. In a 2019 *Yahoo Finance* article, we read:

> Cornell's [Target's 2019 CEO] decision to stay focused on the U.S. isn't surprising, and it makes a great deal of strategic sense. For starters, Target still has a bad taste in its mouth from trying to expand into Canada several years ago. (Sozzi, paras. 4-5)

Lastly, a nonprofit could say that it currently provides free tutoring for 500 children in Chicago and that it would like to add a new program in a major US city each year for the next decade.

On this point, I like to use the metaphor of a five-lane freeway. I once asked a senior team to evaluate their direction and pacing by imagining that there was a five-lane freeway and that their industry was in the middle lane going 65. Some organizations were in the far left lane going 75, while others were in the far right lane going 55. I asked the senior team what lane they thought they were in and they said the far right at 55. I then spoke with a few of their direct reports, who admitted that they were not even in the right lane of the freeway—they were on the shoulder going even slower. They all recognized the need to speed up.

Communicating vector to employees helps give them a sense of where the organization is headed and at what speed. Again, make sure your vector aspirations and statements align with your overall vision and strategy. Vector statements that are routinely unrealized can put a dent in employee morale.

Voice – What Is Your Look and Feel? (Culture)

Microsoft, Google, and Apple are all tech companies. That said, they each have a different culture, which means that their customer and employee experiences are different. Some companies are more casual and fun. Others are more formal. Some companies feel large, while others have more of a family feel.

Voice describes how others experience you. While these are qualitative features, this discussion can be very helpful in describing and building current and future organizational culture.

The interplay between your strategy and culture is critical. As Peter Drucker is famous for saying, "Culture eats strategy for breakfast." Based on my consulting experience, I have to agree with him. Understanding how people experience your organization both internally (employees) and externally (customers) is critical to your strategy and success.

Visuals – What Do You Look Like?

Every organization and company uses visuals in some way, whether through logos, a building, or even the way people dress. The look of your logos, buildings, and people tell a lot about your organization.

You can see the visual contrast between Apple and HP. Apple has more of a casual, California feel while HP has more of an office and tech/engineering feel. When you reflect on the look of your organization, is it communicating what you want to your market?

Other Considerations

Before we move from the highest level of visionary engagement, there are a few other issues that should be considered.

Complex and Distributed Organizations

Smaller organizations may have just one office with one set of employees. Larger organizations and companies may have several divisions and may work in different countries. This often raises questions about multiple mission, vision, and value statements. There are several approaches you can take.

One set of statements for the entire organization – This approach puts a premium on everyone being the same and allows for little or no variation across the organization.

Multiple statements with significant alignment – In this case, an organization may have a single mission or vision statement with multiple values and value propositions, depending on their business line or location.

For example, General Motors makes cars, but they do so in a number of different lines, including Chevrolet, Buick, and Cadillac. General Motors' corporate mission statement is:

> To earn customers for life by building brands that inspire passion and loyalty through not only breakthrough technologies but also by serving and improving the communities in which we live and work around the world. (Panmore.com, 2017)

Buick does not have a separate mission statement, but here is one Buick dealer's mission statement:

> To provide the transportation needs to our community better than any other company by treating our customers, associates, and suppliers as we would like to be treated. (Dutton Buick, 2019)

Broad Collection – Some large holding companies include several companies in different industries and locations. Beyond profit, there may be very little that aligns these various entities.

Each organization must decide:

- How much is the same across various departments and divisions?
- How much diversity and alignment are allowed and expected?
- How much will units be allowed to go their own way as long as they meet certain outcomes?

WHAT TO DO NEXT?

With some work, visionary-level strategic clarity is within the grasp of leaders and teams. You must work through your mission and V6 in collaboration with key stakeholders, who may include any of the following:

- CEO
- Oversight boards
- Senior team members
- Other leaders and employees as appropriate

There are several things teams can do to move forward at this visionary level.

Assess Strategic Clarity

Review your visionary documents and see how much clarity the following groups have:

- Owners or Board
- Senior team
- Directors (direct reports to senior team)
- Working employees

Strategic Leaders Are Made, Not Born has a chapter on the Good-to-Great Rubric. I often use this rubric to assess strategic clarity by asking, "Is our strategic clarity on the following items great, good, adequate, or poor?"

- Where are we headed? (vision)
- What are our current priorities?
- How do we measure success?
- Are our resources and initiatives aligned with our priorities?

If your visionary language is current, useful, and well-aligned, you can move on to the lower levels of your strategy work.

Assess Alignment

Some organizations have great strategic clarity at the visionary level but lack good alignment down through critical measures and the use of limited resources. However, their visionary elements don't impact their decision-making. If that is the case, we will make some suggestions later.

Revising Visionary Content

If your visionary content is not current, useful, or well-aligned, you should consider revising it. Some groups do this revision work, which can take 6, 12, or even 18 months, before they move to lower levels. Other groups appoint a task force to update and revise their visionary language while undertaking lower-level strategy work at the same time.

Communicating Visionary-Level Language

I have worked with many senior teams who spend hours and hours crafting their visionary language only to move onto the next thing. A common problem occurs when 5-10 executives know this language well, but it is not conspicuous to everyday employees.

Start by getting good-to-great strategic clarity at the visionary level. Next, plan to thoroughly and consistently communicate your vision across all levels of your organization over the next 6-12-24 months.

In John Kotter's (1996) book, *Leading Change*, which I highly recommend, he describes Error #4, "Under-communicating by a Factor of 10 (or 100, or even 1,000)" (p. 9). To this end, I recommend what I call the 5x5=50% approach. Let's say that an organization comes up with a new set of three values. I suggest the following plan:

- Choose five channels of communication such as a 1) website, 2) newsletter, 3) email, 4) town hall meeting, and 5) director staff meetings.
- Next, use each of these five channels at least five times each over the next five months.
- As a result, 50% of your people will be aware of your values.

Whenever I share this plan with senior teams, they get discouraged. They complain that it is a lot of work for only 50% awareness. The math is not what is most important here. What matters is the reality that communicating ideas across an organization requires consistent hard work through several channels and on multiple occasions.

I suggest that you develop a robust marketing and educational plan to communicate your crucial strategy elements to all your employees. Many times, senior teams have not considered how to communicate down through their organizations.

Several years ago, I planned to speak to the board of a large organization about their strategy development. As it turns out, I was snowed in and couldn't go. Instead, I developed a 7-minute video and sent it to them. I still remember the president telling me, "Rick, it was better that you weren't here." I thought I was a good presenter, but I listened anyway. She explained that the video was not only passed on to board members (some of whom were also snowed in), it was also distributed to the rest of the organization. Instead of speaking live to a limited group of leaders, my message was shared with many others over an extended period of time.

Since then, I have spent more and more time helping organizations develop materials (emails, podcasts, videos, etc.) to communicate their strategic narrative with their people. I don't have to do this work, but somebody must in order to maximize strategic clarity across an organization.

Strategy Maps

In their book *Strategy Maps: Converting Intangible Assets into Tangible Outcomes*, Kaplan and Norton (2004) developed a powerful visual for use with balanced scorecards called "strategy maps." I have developed these for dozens of organizations. The following diagram shows how to get started. Think of the vision statement as upward and aspirational while the mission, values, and value propositions are foundational. You can also think of the value propositions as the ground floor where customers interact.

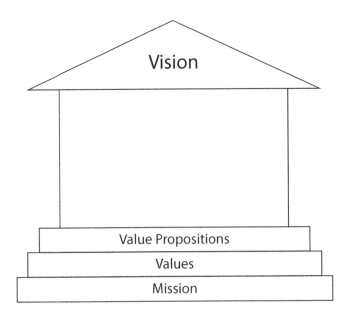

Your strategy map doesn't have to look like a building; nonetheless, visuals can be powerful tools for communicating your strategic narratives.

The Strategy Hand

If you need a quick way to remember these five tools, you can use your hand. Look at the palm of your right hand. Your thumb will be up in the air. The thumb represents MV6. It is at the top, and it is important.

30 MINUTES OF CONSULTING PRACTICE

In every chapter, we want you to get you some real-world practice using these tools. Not only can it be a lot of fun, you can really help people in their lives, professions, and organizations. Let's give you some good questions to practice with.

- Where do you want to be in 10 years? (vision)
- If someone asked you why your organization exists, what would you say? (mission).
- What do you want to be known for? (values)
- What do you provide that others value? (value proposition)
- Where are you today and where do you want to be in x number of years? (vector)
- How do people experience your organization? Are you friendly, formal, organized, chaotic, over- or under-achieving, adverse to change, etc.? (voice)
- What do you wear? What do you look like from a distance? Do you dress formally or casually, hip or dated, in bright colors or pastels? (visuals).
- How well-known are the answers to these questions in your organization?

Asking these questions accomplishes many things:

- You get some practice asking important questions.
- They take time to think about some important topics.
- You get to practice listening.
- They get to see how much alignment their group has on these important topics.

By trying these questions out a few times each week, you will become more comfortable with the coaching and consulting processes. Remember, all of this can be done at the personal, professional, and/or organizational level.

2.

CHOOSING

STRATEGIC THEMES

"The essence of strategy is deciding

what not to do."

–Michael Porter,
What is Strategy?

"What are your 2-3 big deals for this year and next?" I asked the organization's board and senior team. No one uttered a word. The senior team member just stared at the floor.

Breaking the silence, I asked, "Is it not clear at this point?" Everyone quickly nodded. I continued, "Let's see if we can clarify them with this group. It will really help your employees if they know what the big deals are for your organization this year."

You might say that every organization should know their "big deals." Time and time again, however, when I ask the board and senior team of an organization about their strategic clarity, they report that it is poor to adequate. One of the greatest contributions you can make is to help leaders formulate and clarify their thinking on strategic themes.

WHY IT MATTERS

You can't focus on everything. Most people and organizations can only focus on 1-4 high-level areas at a time. You can refer to these as your "big deals." When you gather with others, it is important for everyone to know what the big deals are for this year and next. When people come to work each day, they should have good-to-great clarity on your strategic themes for the next year or two. When such clarity is absent, people lack strategic alignment and tend to go their own way.

HOW IT WORKS

What are your big deals, priorities, or themes? In this book, we use these terms interchangeably. Themes are used more in technical strategy work and refer to 1-4 high-level areas of focus. The timeframe for themes is usually 2-5 years. Most organizations need 2-3 years to advance a high-level theme across their teams, departments, or divisions.

SWOT Analysis

Of the 100 or more themes you could focus on, how do you decide on the 1-4 themes for your organization at this time? First, your themes should be rooted in your mission, vision, values, and value propositions. Second, you should consider both internal and external factors. SWOT analysis has become one of the foundational strategy-making tools for developing themes:

- Internal
  - Strengths
  - Weaknesses

- External
  - Opportunities
  - Threats

For each of the following four areas, you can list 3-5 features.

Strengths

First, look at the strengths of your organization. It is critical to examine your strengths from a realistic point of view. In many cases, insiders feel that their organization has certain strengths, but the markets don't necessarily see the same strengths. Here are some examples of a health clinic's strengths:

- Strong safety record
- Flexible hours after 5 p.m.
- Long-term healthcare providers

Weaknesses

No organization is good at everything. What are your organization's weaknesses? Here are some examples of a health clinic's weaknesses:

- Does not take some insurance
- Equipment is not the most innovative
- Few specialists on staff

Opportunities

As you look into the markets that you currently serve or hope to serve in the future, what opportunities might be worth pursuing? Here are some examples, again based on a health clinic:

- Provide on-site X-rays
- Add a diabetes specialist
- Partner with some area emergency departments

Threats

Markets change, potentially threatening every organization. Here are some examples of threats to a health clinic:

- The clinic is not a part of an area hospital network
- The clinic director is going to retire in a few years
- Patient volume is declining

In a book I co-authored some years ago, *Surviving to Thriving: A Planning Guide for Leaders of Private Colleges and Universities*, my co-author, Joanne Soliday (2014), insisted that we include a section called "SWAT the SWOT." In her extensive experience, most teams do not have the discipline and skill to do a SWOT analysis well. Organizations often overstate their strengths and opportunities while understating their weaknesses and threats. For example, if you ask a college or church about their strengths, they will often say that they are friendly. This highlights two problems. First, most organizations believe that they are friendly and have good service even when outsiders disagree. Second, nearly all of their competitors say the same thing. The results are typically the same: the strengths that you list may not separate you from your competition.

To get the most from the SWOT exercise, you should lean toward understating your strengths and opportunities and overstating your weaknesses and threats. You could have an outside consultant or expert help you with this process, or you can serve as that consultant for others.

Good Strategy is About Tradeoffs

You can't do it all. Organizations attempting too much typically underperform. In his HBR article, "What is Strategy?," Michael Porter (1996) writes, "the essence of strategy is deciding what not to do" (p. 70).

When I first started doing strategy work with teams, I would suggest that they use 3-5 themes. They would often choose five, which is too many for most organizations. Today, I recommend using 1-3 priorities. Patrick Lencioni makes a case for picking just one priority in his 2012 book, *The Advantage*:

Of course, to say that there are too many top priorities is something of an oxymoron. After all, for something to be the *top* priority, it has to be more important than everything else. And even if there are multiple big priorities, ultimately one of those has to be at the very top. The point here is that every organization if it wants to create a sense of alignment and focus, must have a single top priority within a given period of time. (p. 120)

Some of the organizations I have worked with chose three themes and then emphasized one each year, allowing for a broader set of themes while providing focus. Either way, nearly all your people should have good-to-great clarity on your strategic themes for at least this year and next.

WHAT TO DO NEXT

Using a **top-down approach**, take some time to do an inventory of your current visionary language (mission and V6) and documents. You can then assess:

- Do your documents incorporate all the visionary elements?
- Are they sufficiently clear?
- Do you use this language to drive your direction and decision-making?
- Do your visionary elements need to be updated?

NOTE: Even if your visionary elements are not where they need to be, you can continue developing your themes while you update your other elements in parallel.

Next, work through your SWOT analysis to consider which areas may need the most attention.

Finally, collectively list 5-10 possible themes you could use for the next 2-3 years.

You can also take a more collaborative **bottom-up approach**. Bring your people together (everyone or a representative group). Ask them to brainstorm things that need to change. Encourage them to use a verb followed by a phrase. Here are some examples:

- Grow customer base
- Decrease safety violations
- Increase employee retention
- Reduce benefit costs
- Broaden communication

If you have 80 employees brainstorming, you may end up with several hundred suggestions. You can then compile these into 5-10 theme groups.

With either approach, consider using 1-3 words as the label for each theme. Once you have a draft list, prioritize your themes from top to bottom. You can then decide how many themes you want to move forward. As with all your strategic elements, add a sentence or two of description to each theme label. Here are some example themes:

Community Participation – We will focus on growing participation in our programs by expanding community offerings and creating more robust marketing.

Revenue Growth – Entrepreneurial efforts will include several strategies for growing multiple income streams through new program offerings and new locations.

Quality – Program quality will be improved through staff education and advanced analytics.

Safety – An improved safety record will be achieved through employee training and upgraded equipment.

Once you have drafted 1-3 themes, pass them around and see if some wordsmithing is needed. As your themes will be used across the organization for some time, it is best if your collection of themes has a nice ring to it.

Strategy Maps

You can add priorities to your strategy map by using them as columns in your developing building.

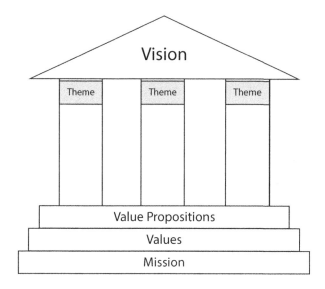

The Strategy Hand

In review, take a look at the palm of your right hand. In the last chapter, we covered mission and MV6, the thumb of your strategy hand. In this chapter, we looked at strategic themes—the index finger of your strategy hand.

Mission
1. Vision
2. Value
3. Value Proposition
4. Vector
5. Voice
6. Visuals

MV6

Strategic Themes (priorities)

Strategic Objectives (strategies)

Strategy Hand

Measures

Initiatives (projects)

30 MINUTES OF CONSULTING PRACTICE

In every chapter, we want you to get you some real-world practice using these tools. Ask yourself or those you work with to write down their 1-4 "big deals." Next week, pass around their responses to see to what extent there is agreement and clarity. This process can be done at the personal, professional, and organizational levels.

3.

CRAFTING

STRATEGIC OBJECTIVES

*"A vision without a strategy
remains an illusion."*

–Lee Bolman,
Reframing Organizations

As a consultant for your team, organization, or others, you can help them craft effective strategies to advance their vision and high-level strategic themes. This process is both an art and a science. The goal is to grow your capacity to craft sets of balanced strategic objectives, helping your teams gain clarity and confidence in advancing their chosen themes. Throughout this book, I use "strategic objectives," "objectives," and "strategies" interchangeably.

For this chapter, I have chosen the verb "crafting" very intentionally. Some of this is from the famous Canadian strategist Henry Mintzberg's 1987 HBR article "Crafting Strategy." He writes:

> Imagine someone planning strategy. What likely springs to mind is an image of orderly thinking: a senior manager, or a group of them, sitting in an office formulating courses of action that everyone else will implement on schedule....

Now imagine someone *crafting* strategy. A wholly different image likely results, as different from planning as craft is from mechanization. Craft evokes traditional skill, dedication, perfection through the mastery of detail. What springs to mind is not so much thinking and reason as involvement, a feeling of intimacy and harmony with the materials at hand, developed through long experience and commitment. Formulation and implementation merge into a fluid process of learning through which creative strategies evolve.

My thesis is simple: **the crafting image better captures the process by which effective strategies come to be.** (p. 66)

Crafting a balanced set of objectives for each theme is at the core of strong strategy development. While themes are higher in strategic altitude, objectives are the lower-altitude strategic elements that drive themes forward. For example, if your theme were "Growing Revenue," you would need to pull together a set of objectives that allow you to move that theme forward with confidence.

Why It Matters

To advance your vision and chosen themes, you will need a balanced set of objectives (or strategies) for each theme. As acclaimed organizational expert Lee Bolman states in the quotation that opened this chapter, "A vision without a strategy remains an illusion." Getting this right is at the heart of good strategy work. Missing the mark can be detrimental on several levels. Richard Rumelt, author of *Good Strategy/Bad Strategy* (2011), writes,

A good strategy has coherence, coordinating actions, policies, and resources so as to accomplish an important end. **Many organizations, most of the time, don't have this.** Instead, they have multiple goals and initiatives that symbolize progress, but no coherent approach to accomplishing that progress other than "spend more and try harder." (p. 11)

In my experience, this approach is common. When I ask teams how things are going, they usually say that things are okay even when they are not. Then, when I ask them about their strategy, they may say something like, "We are going to come in earlier and leave later." Not only does this sound exhausting, it rarely leads to improvement.

How It Works

"Rick, I like you and your vision of this organization," said the board member, turning to face me across the conference table. "I just don't have any confidence that we are going to progress as you have described," he continued.

This board member was an accomplished strategic leader who knew that our strategy was under-developed. I took his words as a challenge. Using the Balanced Scorecard framework, we continued to build a strategic organization that had greater strategic clarity on all levels. This led to the comprehensive advance of our essential outcomes. Developing objectives is mid-level work that is both strategic and aspirational. The goal is to craft a balanced set of objectives that will meet the tests of good strategy.

Porter's Five Tests of Strategy

While Michael Porter is best known for Porter's Five Forces, his Five Tests of Strategy are indispensable for crafting strategy. Porter's Five Tests consist of:

1. A distinctive value proposition
2. A tailored value chain
3. Trade-offs different from rivals
4. Fit across value chain
5. Continuity over time

Keep these tests in mind as you weave together the right combination of objectives. Don't forget to spend time in Chapter 1, clarifying your value propositions for your stakeholders.

Let's move forward by unpacking this mid-level strategic work. Later, once you have a set of objectives in front of you, you can come back and see how they stand up to these tests of strategy.

Mid-Level Strategy Work

To better understand objectives, we want to revisit the concept of strategic altitude. Vision and themes are higher-altitude, more general, and aspirational concepts. Here are some examples:

Vision:
- "Our vision is to create a better everyday life for many people." (IKEA)
- "Build the best product, cause no unnecessary harm, use business to inspire and implement solutions to the environmental crisis." (Patagonia)

Themes:
- "Expand Brand Awareness"
- "Improve Safety Record"
- "Decrease Employee Turnover"

Objectives and strategies often begin with a directional verb, followed by a noun phrase. Here are some example objectives under their related theme:

Expand Brand Awareness
- **Increase** Social Media Usage
- **Train** Employees as Brand Ambassadors
- **Invest** in Brand Awareness
- **Assess** Community Brand Awareness

Strategic Trade-Offs

Above, you read that choosing the right trade-offs is one of Porter's Five Tests of Strategy. A disciplined approach would be to brainstorm and explore the many objectives you could use to advance your theme, realizing that you can't do everything. Choose the objectives that will move the theme forward with confidence and a lower allocation of resources.

Making trade-offs is harder than it looks. Rumelt (2011) explains that bad strategy often results from difficulty making trade-offs. He writes:

> Not miscalculation, bad strategy is the active avoidance of the hard work of crafting a good strategy. One common reason for choosing avoidance is the pain or difficulty of choice. When leaders are **unwilling or unable to make choices** among competing values and parties, bad strategy is the consequence. (p. 58)

While brainstorming helps one see the options, disciplined decision-making is necessary to avoid over-extending everyone in the process.

When leaders are unwilling or unable to make choices among competing values and parties, bad strategy is the consequence.

Label and Description

As you brainstorm possible objectives, develop short labels (2-5 words) and then add a brief 1-3 sentence description of each. Here are some examples that use the objectives listed above:

- Increase Social Media Usage

  Social media usage will be increased by adding more users to more social media platforms and posting daily.
- Train Employees as Brand Ambassadors

  Employees will go through Brand Ambassador training and then be assigned to social media protocols.
- Invest in Brand Awareness

  Brand awareness will be expanded through an integrated marketing plan that includes physical and digital strategies.
- Assess Community Brand Awareness

  A team will develop plans to assess the extent of brand awareness in a 50-mile radius.

Balanced Strategy

The Balanced Scorecard (BSC) framework was developed by Robert Kaplan and David Norton at Harvard Business School over 20 years ago. The Balanced Scorecard has been broadly applied to many industries by many companies. In Kaplan and Norton's 2007 article "Using a Balanced Scorecard as a Strategic Management Tool," they describe how the Balanced Scorecard uses objectives to develop a balanced strategy formed across four related perspectives. These four perspectives are:

- Financial Outcomes
- Customers
- Internal Processes
- Learning and Growth [Organizational Capacity]

NOTE: Like some other BSC Professionals, I have adapted Learning and Growth to Organizational Capacity.

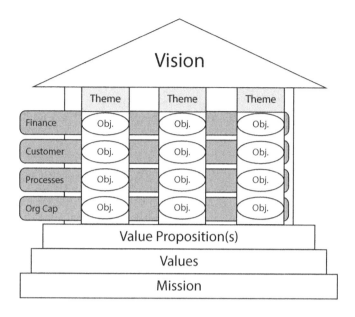

It works well when you develop objectives for each theme that align with the above four perspectives. I have helped many organizations use the Balanced Scorecard and find that these perspectives help ensure that your objectives are balanced. These four perspectives can be visualized with a strategy map, which you can use to communicate the high-level elements of your strategy with stakeholders.

For more information on this, read Kaplan and Norton's (2000) article "Having Trouble with Your Strategy? Then Map It." They also have a full book (2004) entitled *Strategy Maps*. While a strategy map can be a helpful visual for communicating with others, a simple outline can also work well.

- **Theme**: Expand Customer Base
    - ○ **Financial** (Objective): Grow Revenue
    - ○ **Customers** (Objective): Improve Customer Service
    - ○ **Internal Processes** (Objective): Expand Social Media Use
    - ○ **Organizational Capacity** (Objective): Train on Digital Strategies

When I explain this to others, I recommend building the team's organizational capacity first. Then, work to improve internal processes can begin. Finally, ensure that customer-facing service is going well. Progress on these three perspectives inevitably leads to preferred financial outcomes.

OKR Approach

In practice, the Balanced Scorecard framework usually includes all five layers of strategic elements (think of the strategy hand illustration):

1. Mission, Vision, Values, and Value Propositions
2. Strategic Themes
3. Strategic Objectives
4. Strategic Measures
5. Strategic Initiatives

As this process is more thorough, it can take some weeks and even months to design and fully implement.

If you want to use something that is simpler, short-term, and more streamlined for your strategy development, consider adopting the OKR approach.

OKR is a popular strategy approach that pairs **Objectives** (O) with measures that are referred to as **Key Results** (KR). In his book, *Measure What Matters* (2018), John Doerr champions the OKR approach, which has been broadly used by Intel, Google, the Gates Foundation, and many others.

In OKR, the **Objectives** are very similar to the objectives used with Balanced Scorecards. They are broad, directional, qualitative statements that will move you and your organization forward. Most OKR objectives have a horizon of 3-6 months. Ideally, wording will be concise and aspirational (i.e., directional). Here are some examples:

- Improve employee engagement
- Expand online enrollment
- Decrease accident rates

Key Results are quantitative measures that clarify progress on the objective. You will want 1-3 Key Results for each objective. Marissa Mayer, former VP at Google, is famous for saying, "It's not a key result unless it has a number" (Doerr, 2018, p. 14). Remember that the number can expressed as a percentage, raw number, or ratio.

In summary, objectives are mid-level qualitative statements that support and advance your high-level vision and themes. You can use a simple OKR approach that focuses on objectives and related Key Results (measures). Here are some examples:

- Improve employee engagement
    - Employee survey scores
    - Retention percentage

- Expand online enrollment
    - Enrollment numbers
    - Student retention percentages
    - Enrollment growth by quarter

- Decrease accident rates
  - Accidents per month
  - Accidents as a percentage of employees
  - Days out due to accidents

For teams getting started with strategic planning, I often recommend that they practice using the OKR method. Choose a few important objectives and their related Key Results and then run them for a few quarters. You can then expand to a more developed Balanced Scorecard if you want.

In his article, "Using Two-Speed Execution (2SE) to Capture the Value You've Been Missing," Paul Niven (n.d.) explains that the BSC is beneficial for more complex organizations, while OKRs work well for smaller, more agile teams. However, he notes that the two approaches can also be used in tandem.

The BSC is beneficial for more complex organizations, while OKRs work well for smaller, more agile teams.

Structured vs. Emergent Strategy

While Michael Porter of Harvard Business School and many others are from a more **deliberate, structured, planning school of strategy**, there are other schools of strategy thought. Acclaimed Canadian strategist Henry Mintzberg has long championed **emergent strategy**. Emergent strategy focuses on putting strategies into play and then adjusting as needed. Should you use more deliberate, structured planning or should you just move forward and see what results? Yes and yes. On the need for this balance, Mintzberg (1987) asserts that:

In practice, of course, **all strategy making walks on two feet, one deliberate, the other emergent.** For just as purely deliberate strategy-making precludes learning, so purely emergent strategy making precludes control. (p. 69)

This means that you should work hard at deliberate planning, but also learn all that you can in the journey. Your best strategy will come from a combination of deliberate strategy-making and emergent learning.

---

*Your best strategy will come from a combination of **deliberate** strategy-making and **emergent** learning.*

Focus and Discipline

Richard Rumelt (2011) emphasizes that:

Strategy involves focus and, therefore, choice. And choice means setting aside some goals in favor of others. When this hard work is not done, weak amorphous strategy is the result. (p. 59)

Porter (1996) concurs, writing, "the essence of strategy is deciding what not to do" (p. 70)

Focus and discipline are the cornerstones of higher altitude enterprise leaders. I outline these and others in my upcoming 2020 book, *Enterprise Leaders: The First Five FIELD Tools*, which includes:

- FOCUS
- Innovation
- Entrepreneurship
- Learning
- DISCIPLINE

Because many leaders lack the habits of focus and discipline, their strategy never firms up before they are on to the next new idea. Once you have committed to a strategy, be slow to move away from it to the next new thing.

Strategic Time Horizons

Strategies and strategic plans are not perpetual—they need to be updated periodically. Here are some suggested time horizons for editing and updating pieces of your strategy:

- Mission, Vision, and Values (5-10+ years)
- Themes (2-5 years)
- Objectives (review each year)
- Measures (review each year)
- Initiatives (review every quarter)

I suggest both reviewing your strategic plan during a Monthly Strategy Review (MSR) and conducting a significant review each year. A substantial update to your strategic plan should be made every 3-5 years.

Persist or Pivot

Because strategy work is not static, change will come. By holding consistent Monthly Strategy Reviews, you and your team will be able to track progress through your selected measures. On a regular basis, you will have to decide whether you should persist down your planned path or pivot in a new direction. This is both a science and art. The science is analyzing your data and learning from what it is telling you. The art is knowing how long you should persist and how quickly and significantly you should pivot.

WHAT TO DO NEXT

Here are some steps to follow to craft your collection of objectives and your broader strategy.

Begin at the Top

Start by doing a review of these MV6 visionary elements:

Mission
1. Vision
2. Values
3. Value Proposition(s)
4. Vector
5. Voice
6. Visuals

Then, work through Chapter 2 on "Strategic Themes" to determine your 1-4 top themes.

Next, take each theme and begin to build out 3-5 objectives that could move your theme forward. You could use either a loose collection of objectives that seem appropriate or the four perspectives featured on the Balanced Scorecard.

Brainstorm from the Bottom

Don't underestimate the value of getting broad input from your on-the-ground employees. Because they work with these issues day in and day out, they often have insights that management and leadership lack.

On a number of occasions, I have met with as many as 100 or more people and asked them to brainstorm objectives that could move their organization forward. You can then look through the data and see what trends emerge. This process can be invaluable in selecting themes and objectives, especially for organizations that have greater collaboration or shared governance.

One-by-One Development

If you want a simpler approach, choose one theme and then develop a couple of objectives to move it forward. Lastly, read through Chapter 4 to see how you can connect several measures, metrics, or Key Results to each objective.

While it is worthwhile to develop all layers using each of the five tools in this book, it is also helpful to start small. Practice will help you hone the strategic capacity and habits that you and your team will need for the long haul.

Using the Strategy Cycle

Since good strategy work is a learning process, I have developed the Strategy Cycle to help with this learning. The Strategy Cycle is a four-stage iterative process that includes:

- Strategic Thinking
- Strategic Planning
- Strategic Acting
- Strategic Learning

For more on the Strategy Cycle, refer to Appendix A.

Personal and Professional Applications

This tool can easily be applied to your personal as well as your professional life. I suggest you start simple with the OKR approach. It can be powerful to connect an objective in your personal and professional life to a couple of measures (also called metrics or Key Results).

An easy example is weight loss:

Objective: Reduce weight through better eating and exercise.
Key Results:

- Calories consumed each week.
- Minutes of exercise each week.
- Weight on the scale.

The Strategy Hand

Your strategy hand now has:

- Thumb: Mission and V6
- Index Finger: Strategic Themes
- Middle Finger: Strategic Objectives

If you take your thumb, index finger, and middle finger and put them together, you have a powerful combination. These three elements are good for high-level board engagement as well as for a strategy map.

30 MINUTES OF CONSULTING PRACTICE

You now have all the elements you need for high-level strategy development. Take a few minutes and put all three of these levels on a single piece of paper.

4.

TRACKING

STRATEGIC MEASURES

"You can't manage what you don't measure."

–Peter Drucker

When serving as an internal or external consultant, a good question to ask is, "How do you measure progress?" You can continue by asking, "What 5-10 measures tell the majority of your strategy story?" followed by, "Do you review your key measures each month, quarter, or year?" The answer to these questions will tell you a lot about whether things are working or not.

Higher-functioning strategic organizations have greater clarity on what success looks like and the progress being made. You can call these "measures," "metrics," or "key results." Regardless of their name, they are the numbers that offer transparency on what you have agreed on matters most to your organization.

WHY IT MATTERS

You cannot know where you are on your journey if you do not measure your progress. Choosing and using measures that matter is key to clarity, growth, and accountability. While challenging for some organizational cultures to embrace, keeping key measures in front of people is the only way to assess progress and to align scarce resources with agreed-upon outcomes.

When your employees don't know which measures matter, they are more likely to be engaged at a lower level than you would like.

HOW IT WORKS

Measures address a wide variety of topics. Some of them, like data collection, collection cycles and analyses, relate to the math side of the equation. More than you might think, however, are related to how your measures are chosen and how they guide better decision-making. As a matter of fact, this area is sometimes called decision support. Let's unpack some of the key topics in these important areas.

Inputs and Outcomes

Before we get to measures that matter, let's talk about inputs and outcomes. This may be **THE** most prominent issue that I see in organizations. People often confuse work accomplished (inputs) with progress (outcomes). The goal is not more work. The goal is more progress. Say that I exercise for 30 minutes five days a week. While an exercise routine is an admirable goal, it is an input goal, not an outcomes goal. My desired outcome is to keep my weight down as measured on a scale. Exercise is the input that can help me accomplish this outcome. I would not be successful if I exercised all week and gained weight.

A few years ago, I was working with a large organization. We had developed a strategic plan that included specific outcomes as measures and individual initiatives as inputs. As the board meeting approached, I asked the director about the coloring of their themes, which is typically determined by aggregating the colors of the related measures. The most common colors are green for good, yellow for concern, and red for problems. She reported that all their high-level themes and objectives were aggregating up to green. When I asked about the measures, however, she said that they were all yellow and red. I explained that if the measures were yellow and red, the strategic themes and strategic objectives should be the same, as they are the aggregate of measure colors. She insisted that she couldn't justify that coloring because the employees had worked so hard on the initiatives. I acknowledged the input of all the hard work, but noted that the outcomes of the measures had not improved.

I decided not to fight with the director. After the board meeting, I asked the CEO how it had gone. She said, "Not well." The board members had asked why the themes and objectives were colored green even though the measures were yellow and red. They correctly understood that hard work (inputs) does not necessarily mean progress (outcomes).

I should note that there are times when tracking inputs is warranted. For many years, I worked with fundraising professionals. Fundraisers' key outcome is how much money they raise. During times when fundraisers struggled, I tracked their engagement activities, such as visits and proposals. Sometimes it makes sense to adopt blended measures (progress on completed work) that relate to work being done, which is technically an input. As a general rule, however, measures report progress on desired outcomes, not work completed. Work completed will be discussed at length in the next chapter on allocating resources.

Choosing Measures that Matter

Data sets are all around us, which can lead us, at times, to measure things that don't matter. Here are four truths:

- Some things are easy to measure but unimportant.
- **Some things are easy to measure and important.**
- Some things are hard to measure and unimportant.
- **Some things are hard to measure and important.**

NOTE: The bolded lines should have our attention.

The good news is that today, the social and data sciences provide us with the best tools we have ever had to assess both quantitative and qualitative measures.

Quantitative and Qualitative Measures

Most of us are familiar with quantitative measures. We can count the number of people and look at audited financials for the dollars and cents. We can also measure square feet, temperature, and wins and losses. In the event that quantitative data is not currently available for a certain area, it can be gathered over time. The biggest challenge with quantitative data is choosing the right measures to tell the strategic narrative of where you have been, where you are, and where you are headed.

At first glance, qualitative data sets are more difficult. Here are some examples:

- How is morale?
- How did graduation go?
- How was the food?
- Is she a good leader?

There are several ways to get at this kind of qualitative data. For example, you can use any of these tools:

- Surveys
- Focus groups
- Interviews
- Rubrics

Some of these approaches provide an invaluable narrative of what you are assessing. Some can also be translated into numerical data. The Good-to-Great Rubric can help with this.

Leveraging the Good-to-Great Rubric

In *Strategic Leaders Are Made, Not Born*, I spend a whole chapter explaining how to use the Good-to-Great Rubric and the classic 1-5 Likert scale with qualitative data. You can do this informally by going around the room and asking how people felt about a meeting by saying, "How do you feel today's meeting went—Great? Good? Adequate? Poor? A train wreck?"

You can also use a more formal instrument, like SurveyMonkey, to assess statements using the Strongly Disagree — Strongly Agree scale. Provide a statement and offer five choices. Here are a couple of examples:

The CEO is collaborative with others.
- Strongly Agree
- Agree
- Neutral
- Disagree
- Strongly Disagree

The event venue worked well.
- Strongly Agree
- Agree
- Neutral
- Disagree
- Strongly Disagree

SurveyMonkey can conveniently translate the Strongly Disagree-Strongly Agree scale into numerical data for analysis. It is a great jumping-off point for assessing qualitative data.

Operationalizing Measures

When you choose a measure, give it a short, 1-3-word name. Next, add a 1-3 sentence paragraph that makes it clear what the measure is about and how it works. For example, say you work for a college and have a measure called "Retention." You need to operationalize (make clear in operations) what it means. Are you referring to traditional undergraduate enrollment from freshman year to sophomore year? What about graduate students, or retention from junior year to senior year? Clearly laying this out is more important and more difficult than you may think. When people ask me how many faculty members we have in our MBA program at Trevecca, I can tell them how many full-time faculty members we have. I can tell them how many different faculty members (full-time and part-time) teach a course each year. I can list adjunct faculty members as well. Your descriptions should follow this rule: they should be reasonably clear to a reasonable adult. While it is hard to nail down every nuance, you can get pretty close in a few sentences.

Your descriptions should follow this rule: they should be reasonably clear to a reasonable adult.

Framing out Your Measures

With measures, there are several features to work through. You can list measures in a Word document (one or two per page) or an Excel sheet (one per line), making sure to include the following:

- Measure Name (1-4 words)
- Measure Description (1-3 sentences)
- Measure Owner (Who is responsible for ensuring this goes well?)
- Senior Liaison (Who represents this on the senior team?)
- Data Owner (Where is the data housed?)
- Time Frame (Are data sets reviewed monthly, each semester, or annually? On which day are data sets recorded during each period?)

- Data Type (Raw, ratio, percentage)
- Goal (Where do you want to be, and by when?)
- Green to Yellow Threshold
- Red to Yellow Threshold
- Linked Theme and Objective (Strategic alignment)
- Strategic Impact (1-5)

Emotions: Coloring Your Measures

Once you have decided on a list of measures that matter, it's time to determine how you feel about them. I call the next process "data coloring." To facilitate data evaluation, you can use the popular stoplight colors of green, yellow, and red. For every data set, you have to decide where the threshold levels will be.

For example, let's say that you want to exercise 150 minutes per week. Using the scenario above, we could set the following thresholds:

- Green – More than 120 minutes of exercise
- Yellow – Between 90 and 120 minutes of exercise
- Red – Fewer than 90 minutes of exercise

Once you decide upon and implement thresholds you can instantly see how your measures are doing as compared to your established thresholds each month. Don't underestimate the emotions that accompany evaluating your data sets. I like to say that it is just a process while it is still in black and white. Once you assign colors to measures each month, **it can get emotional in a hurry**. Many people will be unhappy if their associated measure comes out yellow or red. This is especially true if your reporting is more public. Data coloring is a worthwhile process, but be prepared for some emotions as you move these processes forward.

*Don't underestimate the emotions that
accompany evaluating your data sets.*

Once, when I was in Chicago for some Balanced Scorecard training, I asked the two people next to me what they did. They said that they worked in the Chicago performance measurement office of Blue Cross / Blue Shield. I asked them about their specific area of focus. They explained that they audited both data and thresholds because when you have thresholds, people often fudge/cheat on their numbers. When an organization begins to regularly, clearly, and publicly report progress, things can get stressful.

I suggest that you start small and practice in private. Practice collecting and "coloring" data before you think about reporting it publicly to your broader teams. Again, don't underestimate the stress and strain this can bring, especially in organizations and teams where this is new.

All Data Is Political

While I like to say that data sets are our friend and are invaluable for helping us improve, they have a political side as well. Many people get nervous when measures close to their work are chosen. While sales and fundraising professionals are accustomed to having data and evaluation around their work, for many others, it can be new and scary. The pressure increases when the process is more public.

*Many people get nervous when measures close
to their work are chosen.*

This doesn't mean that you have to step back from this process. It just means that you should give yourself and your people time to process this level of accountability and transparency. Lastly, don't be surprised if people push back and give you many reasons why you should not do this.

WHAT TO DO NEXT

Using measures that matter can be new for some people and some organizations. Therefore, I recommend starting with training, which could include having others read this chapter or book. You can bring in a coach or consultant to help people work through these ideas more thoroughly.

As part of your training process, make sure your more senior leaders can answer the "why" on this. Why are we taking scarce time to engage these measures? You will have people insist that they are too busy and don't have time for this kind of busywork. You need to have senior leaders who can explain why you are doing this and why it matters. Once people get more comfortable with the concepts, you can then move into the practice phase. This is why you want to start small.

Start with Small Data, not Big Data

There are several issues around using measures and data within an organization. For many, choosing, collecting, analyzing, and reporting data sets are important steps forward. This is often a harder process than you may think. Because of that, I suggest that you begin with just a few measures that 1) people agree are essential and 2) for which you are already collecting data.

Getting a simple start will allow you to work through several key stages:

- Deciding on which measures to use.
- Operationalizing the data definitions.
- Collecting data regularly.
- Analyzing the data.

- Deciding on thresholds for green, yellow, and red.
- Choosing initiatives that will move the needle on your selected measure(s).

Again, it is often more complicated than it looks to develop these practices. Start with just a few measures before you move ahead on a larger number. You might be surprised to see how 8-10 measures can eventually provide you with almost everything you need to assess your organizational progress. You can list 20-30 if you want, but using too many measures can often bring more work and trouble than the value they create, especially in the beginning.

Focus and Discipline

Building and maintaining strategic organizations cannot happen without focus, work, and discipline. I have worked with many organizations that spend a few months developing a strategic plan only to neglect it for the next few years.

Going to the gym to get in shape offers a similar analogy. A personal trainer can come up with a plan for getting fit, but their plan only works if it is put into action. The Monthly Strategic Review (MSR) outlined in Appendix B is a good step forward.

Personal and Professional Applications

As outlined at the beginning of this book, these tools can be beneficial to building the life and work that you desire. Once you have thought through the higher strategic levels in your life and work, you can choose some measures that matter. For me, these include my physical health and professional practice. Some key measures for me include my weight, cholesterol, and my 5K time.

As we have tried to say early and often, we don't want you to win at work and lose in life.

Strategy Hand

Your strategy hand now has:

- Thumb: Mission and V6
- Index Finger: Strategic Themes
- Middle Finger: Strategic Objectives
- Ring Finger: Strategic Measures

This is a powerful combination. Now, you know why you do what you do (Mission and V6), your big deals (themes), and how you are doing (measures).

30 MINUTES OF CONSULTING PRACTICE

List the 2-3 most important measures in your personal life, professional life, and organizational life. In my personal life, I look at my weight, my exercise, and my time with the Bible each day. Every week, I reflect on the time I spend with Cheri. Professionally, I look at the time I have devoted to research and writing. Where is your time going each week?

5.

LEVERAGING

STRATEGIC INITIATIVES

"When a resource is scarce,
you increase its yield."

–Peter Drucker

"Okay, Rick, before you head to the airport, could you just summarize your thoughts from today?" asked the CEO as we stood in the conference room with the CFO and COO.

"Just stop investing in activities with a low ROI and start investing in some new things that will bring a higher ROI," I replied.

"You make that sound so easy," said the CEO.

"It's not easy at all," I explained, "but since every organization has limited resources, it's the most important work that you do."

One of the strategic leader's most important roles is to make the right choices about where to invest resources. Since every organization has limited resources, including time, energy, money, and people (TEMP), precious resources must be invested in those initiatives that will bring the highest return. Strategic leaders are also called on to stop doing things that do not advance what they care about most.

WHY IT MATTERS

Every organization has limited resources. Your focus must be on **maximizing** your results while **minimizing** your investment of resources, which is at the heart of Return on Investment (ROI). Invested resources that don't create results are called "waste." The most critical decisions that strategic leaders make involve how they will allocate time, energy, money, and people (TEMP). Your goal is to allocate the same or fewer resources while gaining the same or higher return on investment (ROI).

Invested resources that don't create results
are called waste.

HOW IT WORKS

While this is the last chapter in this book, it could have been the first, as the principles here are foundational to any endeavor. The key concepts include:

- Return on Investment (ROI)
- TEMP resources
- Outcomes matter more than inputs
- Selecting the right initiatives

While Return on Investment (ROI) has long been a hallmark of the business world, today, ROI is used in almost every for-profit and nonprofit endeavor. One day, I picked up the latest copy of the *Chronicle of Higher Education*, which is like the *Wall Street Journal* for college leaders. On the cover was the question, "What is the ROI of higher education?" At the heart of ROI is the relationship between invested resources and the return on those resources. In other words, when you put in resources, you expect something in return. Many students and their families are wondering about this very issue. In a *US News and World Report* article (2019) entitled, "Gates Foundation Asks: Is College Worth It?," the president of the Gates Foundation is quoted saying, "More than at any other time I can remember, students and families across America are asking themselves, is college worth it?" (para. 2). She adds, "people are actually asking a question I never thought I'd hear, 'Is going to college a reliable path to economic opportunity?'" (para. 2).

ROI questions abound, from colleges to the healthcare and entertainment industries. Is the return high enough for the resources being invested? For those who may be new to the ROI discussion, let's begin with a straightforward personal example. If I go out to a restaurant for dinner, there are some things I expect from my $20-50 investment, including:

- Good and safe food
- Good service
- A pleasant and safe environment

Let's take a more traditional financial investment example. If I put $1,000 into a mutual fund each year, I can hope to get a return of 5-10% or more, which represents the Return on Investment (ROI).

The ROI principle is very powerful and can be used almost everywhere. The goal is to get a higher return on the same investment. You can also seek to invest less and gain an equal or higher return.

TEMP Resources

What are resources? The TEMP acronym is an easy and powerful tool that you can use to help you remember your most valuable resources.

Time: For many people and organizations, time is their most precious resource. That said, many organizations are more concerned about financial resources and often overlook the investment of time by their people. Two kinds of time are at play here. First, there is the timeframe. You could say that a certain project will take three months to complete while another one will take six months. Second, there is the amount of time in man-hours. A project may take 100 man-hours to complete.

Energy: Here, we focus on the effort and attention required to move something forward. In their HBR article, "Manage Your Energy, Not Your Time," Schwartz and McCarthy (2007) highlight that working longer hours does not necessarily generate better results. Effectiveness is tied to the efficient use of your limited energy.

Money: Financial resources are one of the most traditional resources that we track and measure. When we shell out money for something, we expect something in return. This is ROI at its most basic level.

People: People are human resources that are often our most expensive investment. People are very similar to the resource of time but on a larger scale. For one project, we may need 10 hours. For other projects, we may use 14 people for three months. Regardless, human resources are essential to all that we do.

We know that high temps are not good for the human body. In the same way, we should avoid high TEMP initiatives that require a high investment of resources unless we are confident of a high return. A preferred strategy is to choose low TEMP initiatives that provide you with a high ROI.

Outcomes Matter More Than Inputs

Once you understand ROI and TEMP resources, you want to contrast inputs and outcomes. Inputs are invested resources. Returns are the outcomes or results that hopefully comes from those invested resources.

We want to work harder and smarter every day so that we can get a higher ROI from a lower investment of TEMP resources.

Which Initiatives Should We Choose?

Once you understand the principles, you are better equipped to choose the right initiatives. You could do 100 different initiatives, but you probably don't have the TEMP resources for them. Instead, pick the best 5-10-20 initiatives that will bring you and your organization the greatest ROI. Below, you will see how you can choose a better set of initiatives.

When we choose the best initiatives, we have a better chance of advancing our strategy. When we choose worse initiatives, we waste time, energy, money, and people, which is not only unfortunate, it is often avoidable.

WHAT TO DO NEXT

Look at your current investment of time, energy, money, and people and ask yourself what creates the most value and what creates the least value.

Stop Wasting Your Time

Henry Ford once said, "If it doesn't add value, it's waste." This approach is also at the heart of modern lean thinking. In his popular book, *The Lean Startup* (which I highly recommend), Eric Reis (2011) echoes Ford, writing, "Lean thinking defines value as providing benefit to the customer; anything else is waste" (p. 48).

Take some time to write down what you spend your time and money on. Once you have a list of 10-20 items, ask yourself where you should cut and where you should add. Remember, it is a waste of time to spend time on something that doesn't add value.

"Lean thinking defines value as providing benefit to the customer; anything else is waste."

NOTE: In life or any endeavor, there are some requirements that relate to safety and compliance issues. Doing your taxes is a compliance issue.

With that said, there are ways to decrease the time spent on compliance issues in your personal life and within your organization.

Choosing Initiatives

The following is a helpful activity for two reasons. First, it gives you some practice with the methodology, and second, it will help you to make better decisions on where you invest your TEMP resources.

Gather your people together and brainstorm a quick list of 10-20 initiatives that seem like a good fit. I recommend creating a spreadsheet in Excel or Google Sheets. List each initiative on one line and place each of the following features in a different column:

- Initiative Name
- Initiative Description
- Aligned Theme or Objective
- Initiative Owner (Who is responsible for ensuring it goes well?)
- Financial Resources Needed (money)
- Human Resources Needed (time/people)
- Weighted Factors (1-5, 1=low, 5=high)
    ◦ Strategic Impact
    ◦ Compliance/Safety Factors
    ◦ Financial Resources Needed
    ◦ Human Resources Needed
    ◦ A column that is the average of your weighted factors.
- Actual Financial Resources Needed
- Actual Human Hours Needed

Let's say that you come up with the following initiatives:
- Marketing campaign
- HR retention
- Remodel the break room
- Redesign your employee evaluation

Once you come up with a list of initiatives, you can begin to rank them by their average weighted factors. Initiatives that are highest on the list will bring the greatest strategic impact with the lowest investment of financial and human resources (TEMP). The initiatives on the bottom of the list cost a lot but will not add much value.

Once you have decided on your important initiatives, create a mini project charter for each initiative with milestones. You can use a Word document or Google Docs.

Milestones clarify where you should be by when. If you have a six-month initiative, you might have a milestone for each month or two. Here is an example:

Initiative: New Product Marketing Campaign

- Feb 1: Form marketing team
- Mar 1: Present 2-3 marketing strategies
- Apr 1: Begin strategy implementation
- Jun 2: Complete implementation
- Jul 1: Assess results

The Most Powerful Person in the Room

There is a problem that can arise when a group of people comes up with a ranked list of initiatives with items at the top and the bottom. Sometimes, toward the end of this process, the most powerful person in the room decides that despite the data and strategic clarity, they want a bottom-dweller to go forward. There is nothing the other people can do. If this happens once in a while, you can live with it. If it happens regularly, you have a problem that warrants a discussion. Ideally, the best initiatives are those that bring strategic results with a low investment of TEMP resources.

Doing a Premortem and Post-Review

Despite our best intentions, not every initiative or project goes well. The goal of a postmortem review is to learn all you can from what you have done. If you look at the Strategy Cycle found in the Appendix of this book, you will see that it includes:

- **Think**/Talk
- Write a **Plan** or create a Pilot
- **Act** out the plan
- **Learn** from the data

Again, the goal here is to learn all that you can from the wins, the losses, and even the epic fails each time you complete a cycle. This can be challenging because people become invested in initiatives and they can feel bad, even embarrassed, when an initiative doesn't go well. Strategic leaders learn from their wins and losses and get better in the process.

Postmortems are well known. In his HBR article, "Performing a Project Premortem," Gary Klein (2007) discusses the value of looking at critical risks BEFORE a project is selected:

> Projects fail at a spectacular rate. One reason is that too many people are **reluctant to speak up about their reservations during the all-important planning phase.** By making it safe for dissenters who are knowledgeable about the undertaking and worried about its weaknesses to speak up, you can improve a project's chances of success. (para. 1)

You risk sounding negative when you speak out against an initiative, especially if it is being sponsored by a powerful person. We need to provide a safe space for dissent and have the courage to avoid problems that could have been avoided.

Tracking Initiatives

Once initiatives have been selected, they should become part of your Monthly Strategic Review (see Appendix). This means that each month, you should do a quick check in to see whether the initiative is on track and on budget. It does not mean that it is complete, but rather that it has reached the milestone that was agreed upon at the outset.

You can use Green-Yellow-Red coding to quickly make this progress apparent. Green means you are tracking well. Yellow tells you that you are lagging some. Red tells you that you are well off the mark.

When initiatives are not moving the needle on your measures, it is usually due to one of these reasons:

- **Poor Execution**: You may have chosen the right initiative, but perhaps the execution has gone poorly.
- **Wrong initiative:** Sometimes, you choose an initiative that doesn't move you forward.
- **Timing Initiatives:** At times, you may have a lag between the implementation of an initiative and the results that move your measure. This argument can be used for a while, but at some point, it is no longer relevant.

In conclusion, good use of your TEMP resources through the right choice of initiatives is key to strategic leadership. When you choose and invest well, you get more traction on what you care about most. When you don't choose well, you waste resources that could have better been used in other ways. You will not guess right every time. However, through the effective use of the Monthly Strategy Review as well as pre/postmortems, you can engage in on-going learning that can build a brighter future.

Strategy Hand

Your strategy hand is now complete with all five levels.

- Thumb: Mission and V6
- Index Finger: Strategic Themes
- Middle Finger: Strategic Objectives
- Ring Finger: Strategic Measures
- Little Finger: Strategic Initiatives

As your hand is always with you (I hope), it can serve as a continual reminder of your strategic elements. As mentioned repeatedly, the strategy hand can be used for the PPO elements—those found in your personal life, your professional life, and your organizational life.

30 MINUTES OF CONSULTING PRACTICE

List the initiatives in your life and work and see whether they align with your vision and strategy. You should always endeavor to reduce activities that do not produce the value that you want and replace them with higher ROI activities.

CONCLUSION

We opened this book with a conversation about the value you can create for your team, organization, and others by asking good questions and following up with this five-fold process. It is never too early to get started. You don't have to have any particular title or role to ask those around you:

- Who are we and where are we headed?
- What are our big deals for this year?
- What are our strategies for moving ahead?
- What are our 3-5 most important measures?
- How are we doing at aligning our limited resources with our strategies?

START TODAY

Take a few minutes and think about where you could have these conversations. Begin having this conversation with those around you today, tomorrow, or the next day. This practice will help you to gain confidence and it will help others to step away from their tactical tsunami and engage some important strategic topics.

THE PPO APPROACH

Remember the value in starting with yourself. What are the big deals in your life these days? Do your checkbook (remember those?) and your calendar reflect your values and priorities? Recently, one of my adult sons commented on how well Cheri and I were doing in our marriage. I was glad to hear that because, we have certainly had our fair share of struggles in years past. I told him that these days, I do a better job of aligning my TEMP resources with Cheri's priorities. To take one example, Cheri loves to travel. I make sure to block out time in my schedule and set aside money so that we can take several trips each year. And yes, I am enjoying the journey as well.

HOW CAN WE HELP?

At ClarionStrategy, our passion is helping you on your journey. That may involve coaching you as you build your own coaching and consulting skills and experience. It may also be helping you and your organization to grow strategically, Regardless, our continues to be focused on growing stategic leaders and organizations. Whatever your specific needs, we believe that we can help you with them in a way that is affordable to nearly everyone.

BLESSING MORE PEOPLE MORE

For Cheri and me, our mission in life and work is to bless more people more. Some days we are more successful than others. You are also an answer to that prayer. As you go out there and build your strategic organization, you are probably making the world a better place. Know that our blessing and prayers go with you on your journey.

APPENDIX A
STRATEGY CYCLE

In today's VUCA (Volatile, Uncertain, Complex, and Ambiguous) world, we need to be able to quickly and regularly update our strategy and strategic planning. The strategy cycle I have developed here builds on the strategic planning work of John Bryson as well as the lean startup work of Eric Reis. The Strategy Cycle includes:

- Strategic Thinking
- Strategic Planning
- Strategic Acting
- Strategic Learning

Hughes and his colleagues address this, writing "strategic leaders propel their organizations through successive iterations of (make iterations bold) a learning process with strategic **thinking**, strategic **acting**, and strategic **influencing** skills" (2014, p. 4).

With strategy development, there is always a need for regular updates. This is the balance between structured planning and agile, flexible responses to the marketplace.

---

*Strategic leaders propel their organizations
through successive iteration of a learning process.*

Creating Things Three Times

In his classic book, *The Seven Habits of Highly Effective People*, Stephen Covey (1989) says that you have to create things twice, once in your head, and once in reality (p. 99). I contend that in strategy, you have to create things three times using the three creative stages found in the Strategy Cycle:

- Strategic **Thinking** (and talking) – Create your strategic future in your mind and your discussions.
- Strategic **Planning** (and writing) – Next, write down your thinking so you will have a hard copy that you can process with your team.
- Strategic **Acting** – Once you have 1) visualized your strategic future and 2) written down your plan, you can then 3) execute your plan by bringing your thinking and planning to reality.
- Strategic **Learning** – After a chapter of action has taken place, you likely have data sets and measures that can tell you how you are doing. With that analysis in front of you, you can look at the next iteration when you:
  - Re-think
  - Re-plan
  - Re-act
  - Re-learn

This iterative process continues from one activity to the next. Once you have your strategic plan in place, you can continue this cycle again and again. The following graphic illustrates the Strategy Cycle.

Strategic Thinking

Strategic Learning

Strategic Planning

Strategic Acting

Strategic Thinking (and Talking)

The starting point of the Strategy Cycle is Strategic Thinking. This is where you and your team **think** and **talk** through your current strategic elements. Once they are well thought out, you can move to writing them down.

Strategic Planning (and Write)

Strategic Planning involves writing down the fruit of your strategic thinking and talking. Not only does this bring clarity, it allows your key stakeholders to "be on the same page." Remember, you can start with a simple one to three-page draft and continue the refining process through collaboration with others. In some cases, it is beneficial to pilot plans before they are fully implemented.

Strategic Acting

Once your plan has good-to-great clarity, you can put it into action over the coming months.

Strategic Learning

At your Monthly Strategy Review (MSR), look at the updated status of your measures and initiatives to see whether you are making the progress you planned. At this point, you will typically decide whether to **persist** forward or **pivot** in a different direction.

Revolutions Per Minute (RPM)

My initials are RPM (Richard Philip Mann) and I do like active progress. Many organizations review their strategy once per year (annually). In today's world, I recommend a Monthly Strategy Review (MSR). Typically, the higher the RPMs (monthly or quarterly rather than annually), the more opportunities you have for adjustment and improvement.

For example, when I teach an MBA course, I try to improve it every semester. Which professor would you want to teach your course? One who:

- Changes the course every five years.
- Changes the course every year.
- Changes the course every semester.

APPENDIX B

MONTHLY STRATEGY REVIEW

When I ask teams about their strategic planning cycle, I tend to get one of three answers:

- We don't do organized planning.
- We review our strategic planning once a year.
- We review our strategic planning every five years.

In my experience, these approaches will cause your organization to under-perform. At ClarionStrategy, we recommend that teams do a 60-minute Monthly Strategy Review.

Preparing for Your Monthly Strategy Review

About a week out, ask your measure and initiative owners to update their data and colors in preparation for the MSR meeting. NOTE: You may want to assign each theme to a different facilitator. If you have three themes, you could have three different facilitators—e.g. one for finance, one for sales, and one for training.

Affirm Your HIGH-LEVEL Strategy

Begin by taking a few minutes to state and affirm your visionary-level strategic elements, including:

- Mission
- Vision
- Values
- Value Propositions
- Priorities

This process can be done in five minutes or less. Once the elements have been quickly reviewed, make a note of any suggested changes that can be discussed at your quarterly meetings and/or annual review.

Review Each Theme with Its Objectives and Measures

Budget about 15 minutes for each theme. You will spend the majority of your time reviewing each theme's objectives and then drilling down on its aligned measures and initiatives. Here is an example:

Objective – Improve customer reviews
Measures (Key Results)
- Number of Surveys Completed
- Feedback Scores

Initiatives (Resources)
- Customer Service Initiative
- Customer Data Initiative

Annual Review

If you review your measures and initiatives every month, then you will want to review your objectives and choice of measures at least once a year.

3-5 Year Review

Every 3-5 years, you will want to do a high-level review of your visionary documents and your themes.

APPENDIX C
SAMPLE ORGANIZATIONAL PLAN

I often tell leaders that they can put together a simple strategic plan in 3-5 pages. Here is an example of such a plan with three themes.

Educational Tutoring Services (ETS)
ETS is passionate about partnering with parents in providing K-12 students with caring and competent tutoring services at a number of convenient locations and hours.

MISSION AND V6

Mission
We exist to provide quality tutoring services to K-12 students.

Vision
Helping every student to maximize their learning.

Values
- **Personalized** Learning
  Crafting individualized learning opportunities for every kind of student.
- Student **Empowerment**
  Helping students to develop their own individualized learning strategies.

- Partnership with **Parents**
  Providing parents with the tools they need to support their child's learning.

Value Proposition(s)

- **Students** and their families: We provide caring, competent, and personalized tutoring to K-12 students at market prices.
- **Tutors**: At above market wages, we provide part-time tutoring employment opportunities at all hours for those who have a passion for helping students.

Vector

- First Year: 300 enrolled students
- Second Year: 500 students across three locations
- Third Year: 800 students across three cities.

Voice

- Friendly, casual, supportive

Visuals

- Modern, contemporary, and smart casual

STRATEGIC THEMES

Public Awareness

Increase public awareness of ETS through marketing and social media strategies

- OBJ: Expand Brand Recognition
  - MS: Brand Survey Results
    - INIT: Marketing Initiative

- INIT: Brand Survey Project
- OBJ: Leverage Social Media
    - ∘ MS: Facebook Likes
        - INIT: Social Media Training for Tutors
        - INIT: Hire Part-Time Social Media Staff
- ∘ MS: Web Traffic
    - INIT: Update Webpage

Program Offerings

Expand program offerings for both students and their parents.

- OBJ: Expand Student Programs
    - ∘ MS: Student Enrollment
        - INIT: New Student Program
- OBJ: Expand Parent Programs
    - ∘ MS: Parent Enrollment
        - INIT: New Parent Program

Professional Development

Develop tutors through regular, monthly professional development offerings facilitated by development leaders.

- OBJ: Expand Professional Development Opportunities
    - ∘ MS: Tutor hours in development
        - INIT: Monthly development offering
- OBJ: Expand Development Staffing
    - ∘ MS: Development leadership hours
        - INIT: Hire part-time development director

SUMMARY

As you look at this simple plan, note that it has clarified its visionary-level language and put together a functional set of themes, objectives, measures, and initiatives. If this plan were put into action for 3, 6, or 9 months, significant progress could be made. In addition, tutors would know why they come to work (to provide caring and competent services), the three big deals (public awareness, program offerings, and professional development), and how they are doing (brand survey results, enrollment, and development hours). This simple plan can be put together in less than two hours and can provide strategic clarity to the team and drive better outcomes.

APPENDIX D

SAMPLE PERSONAL PLAN

These five strategy tools can also be used in your personal and professional life. Below is a brief personal example using just one theme.

Mission and V6
Strategic Themes
Strategic Objectives
Strategic Measures
Strategic Initiatives
Mission and V6

Mission

I exist to bless more people more across the street and around the world. (Genesis 12:3)

Vision

A growing number of strategic leaders and strategic organizations

Values

- **Developmental**
  People and organizations are in-process and I can support their journey.
- **Empowering**
  Helping others to get to where they want to go.
- **Catalytic**
  Helping leaders to think about what "could be."

Value Proposition(s)
- **Students and Clients:** Helping people to learn and to put that learning into transformational practice.
- **University:** Regularly bringing more value than cost.

Vector
From occasional blog writer to writing one short book each year leader to coach to writer over the decades.

Voice
Friendly, casual, supportive, insightful, and moving forward.

Visuals
Up-to-date, fit, active.

STRATEGIC THEME: HEALTHY LIVING

I want to live a healthy life that is long and strong by staying physically active.

- OBJ: **Healthy BMI**
  After years of an "overweight" BMI, I want to keep my BMI in the "normal" range for my age, height, and gender.
  - MS: **Weight**
    I want to weigh in at least 4 days per week and average a BMI that is 24 or less.
    - INIT: **Daily Weigh Ins:** Buy an electronic scale that syncs with my phone. Weigh myself at last 4 times every week.
- OBJ: **Manage Diet**
  - MS: **Daily calories**
    - INIT: Start using smartphone app for calorie counting.

- ○ MS: **Calories through Drinking**
  - • INIT: Drink water most every time.
- • OBJ: **Learning to be healthy**
  - ○ MS: Pages Read
    - • INIT: Buy and read at least one book per month on healthy living.

SUMMARY

Even one theme can move me ahead in my personal life. I have clarified my high-level visionary elements. I have chosen one theme and built out three objectives to move that theme forward as well as measures that will show me the progress I am making. Is there something in your life that you care about that you would like to move forward? These five tools can help you with that.

APPENDIX E

RECOMMENDED READING

FOUNDATIONAL ARTICLES

Collis, D., & Rukstad, M. (2008). "Can you say what your strategy is?"

Kotter, J. (2007). "Leading change: Why transformation efforts fail."

Porter, Michael. (1990) "What is strategy?"

FOUNDATIONAL BOOKS

Collins, J. (2005). *Good to great and the social sectors.*

HBR 10 must reads on strategy. (2001).

Kotter, J. (2012). *Leading change.*

Lafley, A. & Martin, R (2013). *Playing to Win.*

Lencioni, P. (2012). *The advantage.*

Rumelt, R. (2011). *Good strategy, bad strategy.*

UPPER-LEVEL BOOKS

Hughes, R., Beatty, K., & Dinwoodie, D. (2014). *Becoming a strategic leader.*

Kaplan, R. & Norton, D. (1996). *The Balance Scorecard.*

Magretta, J., & Stone, N. (2013). *What management is.*

Magretta, J. (2012). *Understanding Michael Porter.*

Sloan, J. (2014). *Learning to think strategically.*

NOTE: These resources can all be found in the References section of this book.

SUBSCRIBING TO HARVARD BUSINESS REVIEW

Over 30 years ago, I asked an internationally-known nonprofit leader what I should read. He said, "Read *Harvard Business Review.*" I scoffed at his answer, saying to myself that I wanted to change the world and didn't have the time or the interest to read HBR. In recent years, I went back to that leader and told him how dumb I was. Today, I read every HBR issue cover to cover. The topics covered are much broader than just business. Therefore, when people ask me what they should do if they don't have the time or the money for an MBA, I recommend HBR. For those graduating MBA students who ask what they should do next, I say read HBR. That includes about everyone who wants to grow as a strategic leader.

For about $100 a year, you can get both the paper copy and digital access to current and past articles. HBR offers a treasure chest of insight on many business and non-business topics.

REFERENCES

Beatty, K. (2010, October 27). The three strengths of a true strategic leader. Retrieved December 29, 2018, from https://www.forbes.com/2010/10/27/three-strengths-strategy-leadership-managing-ccl.html

Bryson, J. (2011). *Strategic planning for public and nonprofit organizations: A guide to strengthening and sustaining organizational achievement* (4th ed.). San Francisco, CA: Jossey-Bass.

Bryson, J. M. (2011). *Implementing and sustaining your strategic plan: A workbook for public and nonprofit organizations.* San Francisco, CA: Jossey-Bass.

Bryson, J. M., & Alston, F. K. (2011). *Creating your strategic plan: A workbook for public and nonprofit organizations* (3rd ed.). San Francisco, CA: Jossey-Bass.

Camera, L. (2019). Gates Foundation asks: Is college worth it? Retrieved October 3, 2019, from https://www.usnews.com/news/education-news/articles/2019-05-16/gates-foundation-launches-major-higher-ed-initiative

Christensen, C. (1997). *The innovator's dilemma: When new technologies cause great firms to fail* (Reprint ed.). Boston, MA: Harvard Business Review Press.

Christensen, C., Allworth, J., & Dillon, K. (2012). *How will you measure your life?* New York, NY: Harper Business.

Collins, J. (2005). *Good to great and the social sectors: Why business thinking is not the answer.* New York, NY: HarperCollins.

Collins, J. C. (2001). *Good to great: Why some companies make the leap—And others don't.* Princeton, NJ: HarperBusiness.

Collins, J. C., & Porras, J. I. (1994). *Built to last: Successful habits of visionary companies*. New York, NY: HarperBusiness.

Collins, J. C., & Porras, J. I. (1996). Building your company's vision. *Harvard Business Review, 74*(5), 65–77.

Covey, S. R. (1989). *The 7 habits of highly effective people: Powerful lessons in personal change*. New York, NY: Fireside.

Doerr, J., & Page, L. (2018). *Measure what matters: How Google, Bono, and the Gates Foundation rock the world with OKRs*. New York, NY: Portfolio/Penguin.

HBR's 10 must reads on strategy. (2011). Boston, MA: Harvard Business Review Press.

Hughes, R., Beatty, K., & Dinwoodie, D. (2014). *Becoming a strategic leader: Your role in your organization's enduring success* (2nd ed.). San Francisco, CA: Jossey-Bass.

Kaplan, R., & Norton, D. (2000). Having trouble with your strategy? Then map it. Retrieved October 3, 2019, from https://hbr.org/2000/09/having-trouble-with-your-strategy-then-map-it

Kaplan, R. S., & Norton, D. P. (2007, July 1). Using the balanced scorecard as a strategic management system. *Harvard Business Review*, (2007). Retrieved from https://hbr.org/2007/07/using-the-balanced-scorecard-as-a-strategic-management-system

Kaplan, Robert, & Norton, D. (1996). *The balanced scorecard: Translating strategy into action*. Cambridge, MA: Harvard Business Review Press.

Kaplan, Robert, & Norton, D. (2004). *Strategy maps: Converting intangible assets into tangible outcomes*. Cambridge, MA: Harvard Business Review Press.

Kaufman, J. (2012). *The personal MBA: Master the art of business*. New York, NY: Portfolio/Penguin.

Klein, G. (2007). Performing a project premortem. Retrieved October 3, 2019, from https://hbr.org/2007/09/performing-a-project-premortem

Kotter, J. (1990). *Force for change: How leadership differs from management*. Cambridge, MA: Free Press.

Kotter, J. (2012). *Leading change*. Boston, MA: Harvard Business Review Press.

Lafley, A., & Martin, R. (2013). *Playing to win: How strategy really works*. Cambridge, MA: Harvard Business Review Press.

Lencioni, P. (2012). *The advantage: Why organizational health trumps everything else in business*. San Francisco, CA: Jossey-Bass.

Magretta, J. (2002). *What management is: How it works and why it's everyone's business*. New York, NY: Free Press.

Magretta, J. (2012). *Understanding Michael Porter: The essential guide for competition and strategy*. Cambridge, MA: Harvard Business School Publishing.

Mann, R. (2019). *Strategic leaders are made, not born: The first five tools for escaping the tactical tsunami*. Nashville, TN: ClarionStrategy.

Mintzberg, H. (1987). Crafting strategy. *Harvard Business Review, 65*(4), 66–75.

Mintzberg, H., Lampel, J., & Ahlstrand, B. (2005). *Strategy safari: A guided tour through the wilds of strategic management*. New York, NY: Free Press.

Niven, P. (n.d.). *Using two speed execution (2SE) to capture the value you've been missing*. Retrieved from http://www.senalosa.com/download-my-new-paper-on-two-speed-execution/#

Porter, M. E. (1996). What is strategy? *Harvard Business Review, 74*(6), 61–78.

Porter, M. E. (1998a). *Competitive advantage: Creating and sustaining superior performance* (1st Free Press ed.). New York, NY: Free Press.

Porter, M. E. (1998b). *Competitive strategy: Techniques for analyzing industries and competitors*. New York, NY: Free Press.

Ries, E. (2011). *The lean startup: How today's entrepreneurs use continuous innovation to create radically successful businesses*. New York, NY: Crown.

Rumelt, R. P. (2011). *Good strategy, bad strategy: The difference and why it matters*. New York, NY: Crown Business.

Schwartz, T., & McCarthy, C. (2007). Manage your energy, not your time. Retrieved July 21, 2018, from https://hbr.org/2007/10/manage-your-energy-not-your-time

Sinek, S. (2009). *Start with why: How great leaders inspire everyone to take action*. New York, NY: Portfolio/Penguin.

Sloan, J. (2014). *Learning to think strategically* (2nd ed.). New York, NY: Routledge.

Sozzi, B. (2019). Target won't be expanding around the world anytime soon. Retrieved October 3, 2019, from https://finance.yahoo.com/news/target-wont-be-expanding-around-the-world-anytime-soon-130844268.html

Stolzoff, S. (2019). How do you turn around the culture of a 130,000-person company? Ask Satya Nadella. Retrieved October 3, 2019, from https://qz.com/work/1539071/how-microsoft-ceo-satya-nadella-rebuilt-the-company-culture/

Leinwand, P., Mainardi, C., & Kleiner, A. (2015, December 30). *Only 8% of leaders are good at both strategy and execution*. Retrieved from https://hbr.org/2015/12/only-8-of-leaders-are-good-at-both-strategy-and-execution

Lencioni, P. (2012). *The advantage: Why organizational health trumps everything else in business*. San Francisco, CA: Jossey-Bass.

Lencioni, P. (2004). *Death by meeting: A leadership fable...About solving the most painful problem in business*. San Francisco, CA: Jossey-Bass.

Lloyd Parry, R. (2017). *Ghosts of the tsunami: Death and life in Japan's disaster zone*. New York, NY: Farrar, Straus and Giroux.

Magretta, J. (2012). *Understanding Michael Porter: The essential guide to competition and strategy*. Boston, MA: Harvard Business School Publishing.

Magretta, J., & Stone, N. (2013). *What management is: How it works and why it's everyone's business*. London, England: Profile Books.

McChesney, C. & Covey, S. (2012). *The 4 disciplines of execution: Achieving your wildly important goals*. New York, NY: Free Press.

Porter, M. E. (1990). What is strategy? *Harvard Business Review*, 74 (6), 61-78.

Schwartz, T. and McCarthy, C. (2007). Manage your energy, not your time. *Harvard Business Review*, 85 (10), 63–73. Retrieved from https://hbr.org/2007/10/manage-your-energy-not-your-time

Sinek, S. (2009). *Start with why: How great leaders inspire everyone to take action*. New York, NY: Portfolio/Penguin.

Sinek, S. (2010). *How great leaders inspire action* [Video file]. Retrieved from https://www.ted.com/talks/simon_sinek_how_great_leaders_inspire_action

Sloan, J. (2016). *Learning to think strategically* (3rd ed.). Burlington, MA: Butterworth-Heinemann.

The Thinkers50 Ranking. (n.d.). Retrieved from https://thinkers50.com/t50-ranking/

ABOUT THE AUTHOR

Rick Mann serves as Managing Director of ClarionStrategy, a small consulting firm that develops strategic leaders and strategic organizations that are able to more consistently deliver results and advance their missions. He has worked with organizations in the US and overseas whose annual revenues range from less than $1M to more than $300M.

At Trevecca Nazarene University in Nashville, TN, Rick serves as Professor of Leadership and Strategy as well as the director of the MBA and DBA programs that enroll several hundred new students each year.

Previously, Rick has served in a number of leadership roles in both the United States and overseas, including professor, program director, as well as provost and college president at Crown College (MN).

Rick received his MBA from the University of Minnesota, his MDiv from Ambrose University College (Canada), and his MA and PhD from Ohio State University.

Rick and Cheri live in Nashville, TN. Cheri is a nurse practitioner and works at a clinic for the under-served. Their mission each day is to bless more people more. For fun, they like to work out, travel to that next country, and enjoy the journey together. They have three married sons and a growing gang of grandchildren.

Made in the USA
Las Vegas, NV
13 December 2024

14020785R00069